*Psychic Self-Improvement
for the Millions*

# PSYCHIC
# SELF-IMPROVEMENT
# FOR THE MILLIONS

## THE STORY OF
## CONCEPT THERAPY

*by William Wolff*

PSYCHIC SELF-IMPROVEMENT SERIES

SHERBOURNE PRESS, INC.     Los Angeles, Calif. 90035

# Foreword

For many, this will indeed be the beginning of a new life; a fresh start, a time of fulfillment. Should you wish to learn more about Concept Therapy, I encourage you to drop a post card to the CONCEPT THERAPY INSTITUTE, ROUTE ✳ 8, BOX ✳ 250, SAN ANTONIO, TEXAS . . . Zip Code 78228. You'll receive an interesting packet of free literature and if you wish, you'll be notified of informative lectures to be held in your area.

I don't presume to consider what I have written to be a complete chronicle, but rather I hope it gives the reader an overall perspective to a vast and complex study. Had I more space, I would like to have delved into the lives of other Concept Therapists, such as: Dr. Robert M. Taggart, Dr. Jack F. Schatz, Dr. and Mrs. Charles K. Craig, Dr. William Marth, Dr. C. Harry Roder, Dr. and Mrs. Fred Striffler, Dr. and Mrs. Leon Chesney, Dr. Robert L. Gagne, Dr. Richard Scheetz, Rev. Paul Wilkinson, and many others.

All have interesting and worthwhile experiences, well worth relating; in fact, most every person active in Concept Therapy is worthy of a writer's time and effort. Here are lives dedicated to the proposition that finding the truth and then living it is the most purposeful activity imaginable. To these lifters of life who labor so untiringly in the vineyard of reality, I dedicate this book.

# Contents

*Psychic Self-Improvement
for the Millions*

# CHAPTER ONE

# The Anatomy of an Idea

"No army can withstand the strength of an idea whose time has come," wrote Victor Hugo. Proof of this statement is clearly seen in the world-shaking events in Russia within the last half century.

Several years ago I heard a most interesting talk by Dr. Robert Straus-Hupe, director of foreign-policy research for the University of Pennsylvania. Speaking before college faculties and students throughout the United States, he has skillfully focused attention on a major truism. "America's principle opponents, the Soviet Communists, have one specific asset on their side; it's a secret weapon which we do not possess. This secret weapon is their ability to take ideas seriously."

Dr. Straus-Hupe is quick to remind us that less than fifty years ago the Communist empire measured two feet, the diameter of a coffee-house table in Zurich where Lenin sat as he edited his clandestine newspaper. The weapon with which he defeated a mighty nation's army was nothing more than a pen. That was communism only a half century ago.

Using Lenin's ideas, a handful of men went on to dominate virtually all of Asia and Europe with the exception of a narrow rim of Western Europe and Southern Asia. Eleven hundred million people are enslaved because of the power in just one man's ideas. Yes, it is obvious that the Soviet Communists do take ideas seriously. Do you?

Ideas and the immense power they wield shape our everyday life and redirect our future. They have fascinated me ever since I first became aware that "mere notions and fanciful thoughts" could be a causative factor responsible for bringing about conditions I previously wrote off to chance. If ideas were the stuff of which worlds are created or destroyed, if a mental impression could be the lever to lift one to the summit or plunge one to the depths, then I was determined to understand *why* as thoroughly as possible. A search began that to this day has not ended.

My journey toward understanding started in a lecture room of a downtown Chicago hotel some eleven years ago. Along with a few dozen others, I heard a pleasant, round-faced, heavy-set man with a honeysuckle, Memphis drawl compellingly explain a mode of thinking called Concept Therapy. Admittedly, I came there prejudiced, seething with antagonism and certain that someone would try to sell me a phoney panacea. I was prepared for the worst.

But instead, something occurred that I hadn't counted on. What I heard sank deep and fanned a spark of belief. The motivation prompting me to embark on what metaphysical literature refers to as "The Path of Attainment" was neither intellectual curiosity nor (apparent) spiritual hunger, but rather a desperation born of frustration and a feeling that life need not be a vale of tears.

And so I began an adventure of great promise. At my present vantage point, I can honestly say that I was not disappointed in the least. My greatest expectations were realized and the light of truth, ever so dim in the beginning, became brighter with each morsel of knowledge gained. In the pages to follow, I hope to recapture the spirit of a momentous personal experience. With all my heart, I want to share this with you truthfully and free of distortion. It is hoped, that in the relating of this personal involvement, an accurate picture of a dynamic and far-reaching philosophical movement, concept therapy, will come into sharp focus.

You'll meet Thurman Fleet, an unusual man relatively unknown to the world at large but destined, I believe, to become a legend in our time. The story of his unique life's work may forever affect your own daily pursuits and influence your thinking as it has thousands of men and women throughout the United States and Canada.

There are others, too. Crump, Wright, Schenk, Calhoun, Whittenberg, Higdon and a handful of others whose true-life dramas will leave an indelible impression on your thoughts and perhaps provide a beneficial stimulation prompting you toward the heights of self-fulfillment.

Most of all, the words here are intended to provide a workable method of how best to use your own ideas as a powerful magnet that irresistibly draws to you what is most needed and conversely instructs you how to permanently stop attracting conditions that limit your life. That's not all. I will attempt to explain the principle which activates this magnificent mental machinery. One of the keys to Concept Therapy's success is that it asks you to accept nothing on *blind* faith; rather it encourages complete understanding of what is happening and why.

At this point, I must warn: however admirable positive thinking is, I am referring to an aspect far beyond that rather limited, single dimension of the multifaceted scope that is mind-power. There is no denying that a proper mental attitude is important, but it's my intention to illustrate how a person may believe he is thinking positively and still be negating any constructive thought-energy by unconscious actions. The analogy being, taking one step forward and two back. Many a "truth student" has done just that and wondered why his affirmations for health or wealth did not materialize no matter how positive his thinking was.

The difference between an hallucination and an image must be understood, otherwise the reader who attempts to heal (and

I use that word in its broadest sense) with ideas will discover that he will instead be engaging only in pleasant daydreaming or "escape" excursions into flights of fancy. There is a vast difference, indeed, between imaging and hallucinating, because we intend to act on the images. It is just this ignorance of basics that leads to failure when the novice attempts to work miracles by just some "good thinking."

An explanation of what the words "Concept Therapy" mean is called for at this time if we are to proceed properly toward our stated goal. Thurman Fleet defines *concept* as "an abstract general notion or an idea." In Concept Therapy it means *an idea in the consciousness of man. Therapy* means *having healing qualities.* A concept, or an idea, which has become fixed in the consciousness may be true or false, constructive or destructive. Concept Therapy concerns itself with changing faulty concepts in the consciousness. It teaches a method by which false concepts may be discovered, understood, and removed or replaced with true concepts.

In my case, the damaging concept or idea was a feeling of unworthiness. Deep down was a vague notion that I wasn't a very capable person. This generated an overall lack of confidence that was further aggravated by the problem of obesity. To counter this terrible, ego-destroying syndrome, I became an obnoxious extrovert, loud-mouthing it all over the place to cover inner inadequacies. I was trapped in a vicious circle that brought more and more heartache in its wake.

Even though I was grossly overweight, I couldn't continue any sensible diet because I didn't believe I had the needed will power to resist the temptation of fattening foods. Later on I will touch on a vital point that is almost always overlooked by people trying to break a habit. I will reveal the concept that can conquer your unwanted habits. Yes, you can actually enjoy adhering to a strict diet. You can stop smoking and like it. It all depends on what idea you really give yourself. This will all be explained in detail.

Concept Therapy is not just another variation of the "couch

14

and free association" technique. Its teachings encompass a vast panorama that majestically includes the entirety of *all* things. It must and can do no less if it is to successfully instruct man to become a creator instead of a puppet forever enslaved to an association of ideas. That is why Concept Therapy begins its instruction with the UNKNOWN POWER—the source of all created things and, ultimately, of all ideas and concepts.

I can remember, as though it were only yesterday, when I first heard Reverend E. L. Crump (now dean of the Concept Therapy Institute) explain, "In teaching a subject it is essential that we begin with a premise upon which we all agree. As Concept Therapy begins with the creation of the world, we resort to the only two authorities available to us; namely, science and theology."

Dr. Crump was admirably equipped to properly examine these two avenues of man's knowledge. He had graduated from college with a degree in electrical engineering and later worked beside the great genius, Charles Steinmetz. Feeling unfulfilled and in need of answers that science could not give, he went back to school and in due time took his degree in theology. For many years he served as a Methodist minister in Southern pulpits. He earned the love and respect of his congregations but still he yearned for something he could not identify.

His keen, inquisitive mind never ceased its quest for answers—answers that even the church could not provide. Then he discovered Concept Therapy and for a third time changed his career. This time he found what he had been seeking so long. His story is intimately wrapped up in the growth of Concept Therapy and we'll delve into his life in a later chapter detailing the pioneer instructors who devoted their all to bring this knowledge to the world.

During my initial exposure to this philosophy, I recall Crump pointing out that the entire material universe is constructed of small particles of matter called *electrons*, and that from the electrons the world was created. "Science neither

15

admits nor denies the existence of a Supreme Being. It merely states that the existence of God cannot be proved by scientific means. Theology teaches that God created the world either from Himself or from nothing," he drawled in his disarmingly homespun manner.

Echoing the words of Concept Therapy's founder, Crump continued, "The human mind, being taught that for every effect there must be a cause, is unable to accept the premise that something can be created out of nothing. Such a proposition violates the dictates of right reason. Therefore, we are able to consider only two causes; namely, electrons or God."

I sat upright in my chair. I hadn't given it much thought until now, but the words had awakened something within. I was beginning to get more and more interested in the hypothesis presented. I listened more intently as the lecture proceeded, "A careful study will show that there is no conflict between science and theology. Both say the same thing but in a different way. If it be true that God is everywhere, then He must have been in the electron of science."

I could see what he was getting at and I became impressed by this approach that dissolved the need for science and theology to be in conflict. In this day and age when there is a tremendous emphasis on scientific education, a philosophy of life is needed that retains the wisdom of age-old truths, yet is still palatable to an overly sophisticated generation. Whether you're a religionist or scientist, you can start at either of the two causes of creation, and by a process of logical reasoning you will arrive at the same conclusions reached in Concept Therapy.

I've seen it happen time and again where an agnostically inclined husband with a spiritual wife will for the first time have a common foundation of understanding after completing the basic Concept Therapy course. In what adds up to about 25 hours of instruction given over a weekend (Friday from 7 P.M. to 10 P.M. Saturday and Sunday from 9 A.M. to 10 P.M. with a ten-minute break on the hour and time out for lunch

16

and dinner) a new dimension will have been added. Many a marriage that was tottering on the brink of a breakup, has been saved because a line of communication was established. It is just this reason why the Concept Theory Institute does everything possible to encourage husbands and wives to take the class together. A special financial consideration is given if they do.

I can speak with some authority on this matter. A year after my wife and I had returned from Europe, where I was stationed as a Broadcast Specialist with the American Forces Network, we realized that even though we were still deeply in love, divorce was a distinct possibility. My inner torments carried over from childhood and her own unresolved problems had driven us nearer and nearer to permanent separation.

Naturally, this tension and stress caused a detrimental physical reaction and my wife bore the brunt of it. Not only did she endure the agony of a miscarriage, she suffered chronic backaches that would have incapacitated an ordinary woman. But not June. She had a fine spiritual background and an intense desire to make the marriage succeed despite tremendous odds. She has always believed that in nine cases out of ten, the woman either makes or breaks the marriage.

I had come from a broken home. June and I were of different religions. Actually, I considered myself without a religion, rejecting (unfairly) the faith of my parents as something primitive and unusable. Frankly, the example they set was something less than inspiring.

There were other differences, too. I was city bred and my wife raised in a small town. I enjoyed the excitement of the bright lights while she preferred the quietness of nature. Add to this all the other burdens of personality defects and it doesn't come out as a good bet for a permanent relationship. I used to be surprised at how many people get divorced. Then when I took a good, close look, I marveled at how many people managed to stay married.

As time passed my wife's pain increased. When all hope for

help through medical means had been exhausted, my wife, at the insistence of her mother, sought aid from a chiropractor. After six weeks of treatment, consisting of manipulating the sacroiliac region of the spine, plus a proper diet, she began to feel much better.

The healer, sensing that an emotional adjustment was needed as well as a physical one, dropped a few guarded hints about a forthcoming informative lecture on Concept Therapy. My wife was immediately interested, and on a memorable Wednesday evening she and her mother drove forty miles to attend the lecture.

Afterwards, when she tried to explain about it to me, I was adamant in my rejection of the idea that it could help us. June persisted. We had to do something quickly to save our marriage. On that point, we were in complete accord and so, when another lecture was scheduled, I was there.

My hostility turned to an interest which soon became hope. Rev. Crump ignited a desire in me. All of a sudden, I desperately wanted to gain a working knowledge of CREATION. Imagine *me*, wanting to know how to use the methods of the *unknowable* to create things, thoughts, and acts of a positive, constructive, and beneficial nature. Could I actually do it? Could anyone do it? Was I fooling myself? I had to find out.

We signed up for the class. I was only making fifty dollars a week as a writer and producer of educational radio programs for the Chicago Board of Education, but I could not afford to pass up this opportunity. One thing struck me as being very fair. Katherine Calhoun, Rev. Crump's assistant, made it very clear that if I was not completely satisfied with what I was taught, then on Sunday evening at the conclusion of the class, I could take my check back without any questions. "You mean this course is 100 per cent guaranteed?" I asked. "Yes," came the answer.

Never, ever in all my life had I spent a more worthwhile $150. (The cost for my wife and me.) When the last period of instruction came to an end on Sunday evening, I *knew* that what I had heard was all true. I had received answers for questions I wasn't equipped to ask. It was only the beginning, that was for sure, but at least I had begun.

# CHAPTER TWO

## Ideas in Action

Through the pioneering work of Drs. Harold G. Wolff and Stewart Wolf, science has proof that anxiety is the emotion most damaging to the stomach and is clearly linked with the formation of ulcers. Their experiments proved that when one is calm and at ease, the stomach is pale pink, relaxed, and has many convoluted folds; but it is bright red, tense, and smooth when the person becomes angry.

Three Soviet scientists report that neurotic female mice are more likely to contract breast cancers than mice with healthy nervous systems. Mice who suffer nervous overstrain are more susceptible to cancer, said the doctors in a report to the seventh International Cancer Congress in London.

A Los Angeles psychiatrist, Dr. Leo Rangell, Clinical Professor of Psychiatry at UCLA, reported that bacteria and other minute organisms find it easier to infect people who worry and fret. "All organic diseases are influenced by psychological factors," he said at a post-graduate seminar on psychiatric problems in general practice. "Resistance to infection is influenced by the psychic state," the doctor announced. "A person actually invites bacterial invasion by being emotionally irritated."

During the National Rural Safety Conference, sponsored by the American Medical Association, Albert A. Lorenz, M.D., pointed out, "Depression is a contagious illness that goes on into the second and third generations on farms."

Dermatologists report that a teenager's "frame of mind" plays a major role in worsening an acne problem. Talking over their problems more freely can help clear up their skin.

In the *Journal of Dental Abstracts,* Dr. Philip R. N. Sutton of Melbourne, Australia studied 169 patients over the age of twenty-five who suffered from acute tooth decay. He found that 96 per cent had undergone severe mental stress. Their main reasons for worry were personal or family illness, housing conditions, and business, financial, or employment trouble.

Some years ago, newspapers ran the account that Prince Charles of England's attack of appendicitis might have been caused by suppressed fears. What possibly could this royal youngster be afraid of? For one thing, he was very aware of the strict discipline he would face at Gordounstoun School. Many medical authorities say that appendicitis can be brought on by just such emotional upset.

Dr. Sanford Lewis, internist in charge of psychosomatic medicine at United Hospitals of Newark, N.J., said the intestine, of which the appendix is a part, goes into spasm during emotions of prolonged high intensity. "Emotional upset may cause appendicitis to develop. Otherwise, the appendix may become inflamed but returned to normal."

The condition called senile dementia, or senility, is responsible for memory loss and disorientation in many elderly persons. It results from the slow dying of brain cells. No one knows the exact cause of this deterioration but Dr. V. A. Kral, head of the old-age unit at McGill University, Montreal, believes he has found a clue.

While examining the elderly he discovered that the saliva of the brain-disease victims contained more salt than normal patients. He believes the salt is an indication that the "stress" glands (adrenals) of dementia patients are working much harder than in the normal person.

Whether the inability to adapt to stress is hereditary or environmental is not known, but Dr. Kral's study indicates that a stress-filled childhood is the trigger that sets off chemical imbalance resulting in brain-cell deterioration. So wrote *Los Angeles Times* medical editor Harry Nelson in a report covering a 1964 meeting of the Society of Biological Psychiatry in Los Angeles.

"Asthma is purely psychological and isn't even a disease—it's a symptom," says Dr. A. Philip Magonet of London. "Climate has nothing to do with it, nor do allergies or colds or bronchitis. It's all a matter of tension." A United Press International report said the British doctor claimed that all the adult asthmatics he has dealt with were introverted and appeared shy, sensitive, anxiety prone, perfectionist, and obsession filled.

I have literally hundreds of such references in my files clearly illustrating the immense role our thoughts play in determining our health. Fear, anxiety, tensions, and nervousness may all be triggered by false concepts. In other words, a bad idea can cause real, physical harm. But, if an idea can do that much damage, and I have presented what I feel to be a convincing case, then the opposite must be true.

A May 12, 1955 Associated Press dispatch datelined Wichita Falls, Texas, headlined the story of a wheelchair patient who was able to walk again following a "miracle." The attractive twenty-two-year-old wife of an Air Force sergeant said she had been confined to a wheelchair ever since she was hurt in an automobile accident. Her major injury was a broken leg. Twenty months later, she contracted polio and was paralyzed from the waist down by meyelitis, an inflammation of the spinal column. Then one spring day, "something told her to walk"—and she did.

Her minister called the woman and her husband a deeply religious couple. He attributed her reported recovery to "constant prayer and belief in the healing power of God." Faith cures are legion. Always, stories of new ones keep cropping up in our newspapers and magazines.

McCandlish Phillips, in the *Saturday Evening Post,* wrote an excellent article on the practice of praying in "unknown tongues." Reported were cases of at least six men who became instantly relieved of afflictions of long standing. The article quoted Baptist Rev. Howard Ervin.

"We saw a blood clot disappear immediately. An appliance repairman who had torn cartilages in both knees was healed instantly. He could barely walk when he came in for prayer, and afterwards he *ran* down five flights of stairs to his car. He was absolutely free," the Preacher said.

Henry S. Huber, M.D., Attending Surgeon, French Hospital, New York and Visiting Surgeon, City Hospital, Elmhurst, N.Y., wrote in *This Week Magazine* of April 15, 1962, "We do not know the physical mechanism by which one patient's will to recover actually helps him to get over a disease to which a pessimistic person succumbs, but that does not invalidate the clinical observation of many physicians—that a desire to get better will assist and hasten recovery."

The mechanism he and his colleagues are unfamiliar with (and this will surprise them) is well known to Concept Therapy. It is, in fact, the reason Concept Therapy came into being. Dr. Thurman Fleet, the founder of this philosophy of life, became aware of a nonphysical element in the functioning process of the body and became a dedicated searcher determined to more fully understand its mysterious workings. How he succeeded and the dynamic implications of his discovery will be detailed in chapter four.

What is it worth for you to learn how to better defend against thoughts which may cause cancer, ulcers, severe tooth ailments, appendicitis and the like? Could you put a price tag on the ability to instill an idea in your child, spouse, parents, relatives, and friends that would call forth a dynamic power able to sweep away pain, and premature bodily disintegration? There are those who are willing to drop preconceived notions, to step on "sacred cows," and to sincerely apply themselves in order to understand this tremendous secret. You'll find them in Concept Therapy classes. They are an uncommon lot.

Many a "mental" or "spiritual" healer, along with doctors, sitting in on a Concept Therapy class have been dumbfounded with the utter simplicity of the explanation demonstrating just why their particular healing methods have sometimes failed. "It always mystified me why some of my people responded so wonderfully while others didn't," a well-known practitioner told me. "After all these years I have finally discovered the reason. Now I know what happens when a cure is made regardless of how it is performed."

An M.D. of considerable importance, during a Concept Therapy informative lecture he was giving at his home, told a group of his peers, "This work strips away the mumbo-jumbo that has relegated an invaluable area of understanding, the power of suggestion, to superstitious clogged cults."

Several years later this same doctor at another informative lecture, this one in the Beverly Hills home of a Los Angeles manufacturer, revealed how his Concept Theory instruction had greatly aided him in all facets of his personal and professional life. "It has also made me an expert medical witness in court trials requiring my testimony," he informed a corporation lawyer who had presumably come that evening to hear about the philosophy but, as it turned out later, really wished to belittle it.

"Now really doctor, how could anything other than what knowledge you have already gained in medical school and as a direct result of your experience as a physician do that?" the lawyer cross-examined.

Retorting, the good doctor said, "You ask what I could learn that I wasn't already taught? For instance, the Composite Personality."

The "legal eagle" looked at him quizzically. "I've never heard of . . . what was that you said, Composite Personality?"

"I'm sure you have," the doctor pressed. "You've read about it in books, in newspapers, and in magazines. In fact,

24

lately it has become quite a popular subject, even among lay-men, *especially* among laymen. People who don't know what they're talking about call it hypnosis. But it is really the Law of Gender and the Principle of the Composite Personality that they are referring to."

The lawyer was visibly surprised. He wanted to hear more. The doctor obliged. "I had four years of psychiatry before specializing in another field of medicine. As you can imagine, I have witnessed a good many hypnosis demonstrations and have heard many lectures on this subject. Until Concept Therapy, I didn't really know what hypnosis was all about."

The lawyer put his scotch-on-the-rocks down and listened. Continuing, the doctor said, "The lesson on the Composite Personality taught me what conditions are necessary to sink a suggestion into a patient. A mother learns how to give her child a suggestion that will be carried out and a salesman learns how to properly give suggestions to a customer. The same principle applies. I also learned, and this is most important, how to avoid suggestions from, say, sharp, highly skilled trial lawyers who during witness-stand examinations will try every trick in the book to discredit the opposition's witness."

"Forget about how it works in my field," the counselor said. "What about in curing the sick? How can this 'pseudo science' teach you something valid that you didn't learn in your formal education?" That question has not only been asked of a few M.D.'s and psychologists but of innumerable chiropractors and religious healers by the hundreds. How, indeed, could this vital knowledge not have been made available in institutions of higher learning?

But let us be specific. What is it we are asking? First, we point out that Concept Therapy for the past thirty-one years has been teaching what suggestion can do in relation to health and exact methods to utilize suggestion in healing. The question then is how is it that great universities have overlooked this tremendously important area of study? Our lawyer friend demanded to know how it was a doctor could learn about the power of suggestion in Concept Therapy and not in medical school. His question was well taken.

The doctors themselves are concerned. Henry K. Beecher, M.D., of Boston, writing in the *Journal of the American Medical Association* (November 30, 1963) points out, "In recent years increasing awareness of the power of suggestion, the power of placebos, the importance of nonspecific forces surrounding disease and the treatment of disease, evidence that extreme anxiety can kill—all these things have led to the conviction that certain supposed results of specific therapy may in truth be consequences of suggestion."

Please don't jump to the erroneous conclusion that all sickness can be healed via the suggestion route. Concept Therapy imparts an understanding of why all healing methods must sometimes fail and why even some scientifically doubtful "shenanigans" are seemingly so successful. Writing on the subject, Dr. Fleet informs, "Medicine, chiropractic, osteopathic and naturopathy are physical sciences which treat or work on the body to alleviate disease. Each has its merits, and each has a place in healing. Each also has its success and failures. But, when confronted with a disease which has its origin in the mind, all fail to bring about a cure. They fail because they are treating EFFECTS when the CAUSE lies in the mind.

"Psychiatry, psychology, psychoanalysis, psychotherapy, Christian Science, Science of Mind, Unity, etc., are mental sciences which treat, or work on the mind to alleviate, disease. There is no question that these systems do cure a great many people. But when attempting to treat a disease which has a purely physical origin, they also fail—unless those who use the methods understand the great secret behind all healing.

"Concept Therapy presents the methods of effecting cures under any and all systems. The PRINCIPLE underlying all healing is made clear. One who understands is then able to eliminate disease on all three planes—physical, mental, and spiritual."

Many a person would get "hot under the collar" when hearing Fleet say, "It's erroneous to think or believe that one must become religious, change his religion, or engage in any religious work in order to use this Principle. Quite the opposite is true. Concept Therapy works strictly along a scientific basis involving an understanding of the Law."

It is just this that attracts so varied a group of searchers to Concept Therapy's fold. The agnostic can comfortably sit beside the "believer" and both can benefit, each to the limit of their evolvement. "Praying for someone to get well is fine; nothing wrong with it," Fleet allows. "But it is far better to know the Laws and to work them to obtain the desired results. Positive affirmations are okay but right action is much more effective."

If Dr. Fleet comes off a little irreverent at times, it's because he means to do just that. He has little patience with metaphysical phonies, especially those who prance about spouting Biblical passages so as to lend an air of authority to their fantasies. To make a point, he will often resort to an analogy simple enough for anyone to comprehend.

"Nobody," he says, "in their right mind would prostrate themselves on the floor in front of an electrical outlet in hope that their worshipful attitude would make it light up the room. That would be nonsense. Instead, they'd go get a lamp, plug it in, and turn it on. If the thing didn't work, they would either figure that the bulb needed replacing or some connection wasn't just right. They most certainly wouldn't for a minute think that the Laws of electricity are at fault."

Dr. Fleet has another unique characteristic that brings a smile to the lips of those familiar with him and his methods. It's his manner of speaking. "Nobody can 'murder' the 'King's English' like Fleet can, when he has a mind to," explains Bernie Higdon. Dr. Higdon, a veteran of the movement from the early days, is also not surprised when Dr. Fleet will *ad lib* an hour talk on some deep philosophical subject in flawless grammar. Katherine Calhoun, another instructor, sometimes acts as his secretary. "Many times he'll dictate page after page, including every period, comma, semicolon and quotation mark . . . all the punctuation and all correct."

But as interesting as is the man, at this point our attention is primarily focused on the work. We will have time later in the book to really become acquainted with Dr. Fleet. However, it is almost impossible to refrain from bringing him in at various junctures and we will do so whenever the situation calls for it.

There used to be a television commercial that said, "Take tea and see." It seemed to strike a respondent chord in me. This is the reason. Everytime I was confronted with some unpleasant situation that needed facing, I took "tea." Not the beverage but the . . . how can I properly describe it . . . reminder, I guess . . . my own personal memory device. Because the three letters reminded me of the only possible action available.

The first letter T stood for transmute. E represented eliminate and A, well I'll save that for the "punch line." Now, to explain. When I had a problem, a serious one, I would generate a lot of morbid energy because of it and I would do myself a lot of inner damage by continuing this line of thought. What to do?

The realization that I had only three possible courses of action finally popped into my mind. I could transmute the problem, change it, that is. Or I could maybe eliminate it. Now if I couldn't do either of the aforementioned, then all I could do would be to ADAPT to it. With this understanding I immediately stopped my "stewing" and determined which one of the categories I could most logically utilize. One of the hardest "pills" to swallow is the cold, unhappy fact (and so often facts do appear unfriendly) that the only thing to do would be to adapt when I would so much rather transmute or eliminate.

Sometimes what appears to be negative to us is in reality very positive. That's not an excuse for failure, really. Constantly trying to eradicate the bad is not a very desirable mode of action. Even though this book in part is aimed at enlightening you on the methods used to get what you want, be it known here and now, happiness does not come from living in an "ivory tower."

True, you must not suffer poverty, but having your happiness dependent on getting everything you want, having all your wishes come true and avoiding all frustrations, is a one-way street to "woesville." The alcoholic and drug addict are prime examples of a type not able to cope with the illusions of life. They think they see ugliness, and in striving to avoid something that would make them feel bad, they sink deeper into the "pit."

I'm reminded of the following: You must have both negative and positive electrical energy for the light bulb to glow. The analogy being that experiences we dub negative or bad and positive or good are both needed if we are to become illuminated. That is, to see life as it really is and not through illusions that cloud the vision, many experiences must come our way.

Something the usual run-of-the-mill inspirational, mind-power books dare not tell you is that you can become addicted to positive thinking. By continually blotting out that which is not "rosy" or just to your liking, you will become more and more dependent on a life style that must finally disable you. The most subtle of all dangers is the unconscious, yet powerful suggestion we drive deep down every time we avoid accepting life's challenges. Some kinds of escapist thinking are as much crutches for the spiritually crippled as is drinking.

Of all the lessons that Concept Therapy teaches, most important to my way of thinking is ADAPTATION. Not only did I learn the significance of that ancient admonition carved thousands of years ago on the temple at Delphi, "Man, know thyself," but I was taught how to constructively cope with negative factors in the personality of others as well as my own and also in my environment. This enabled me to find peace without resigning from the active world.

The above is not just one man's story. It is the same with thousands and thousands of others. To be a bit more specific, fifteen thousand men, women and even children have enrolled in classes. An overwhelming majority have benefited enormously. A high percentage wishing more knowledge on the subject continue their instruction in advanced Conceptology classes.

Some, having secured enough understanding to solve specific problems, feeling no more need to study, cease further investigation. There is nothing compulsory about it. Six years ago I chose at random a hundred names of those who had taken Concept Therapy in the Los Angeles area. I sent them a questionnaire. Ninety-five per cent of my returns (eighty-five sent answers back) admitted that they received what they had enrolled for and had high praise for the work. Interestingly enough, these were people who had dropped out of local study clubs and had severed all ties with Concept Therapy. Even their consensus was that it was a most valuable teaching.

The truths regarding the great unknown power and the Laws of Life are not the revelation of any one person. Dr. Fleet is the first to make this clear. What Concept Therapy does, is to present in simple, understandable language, the *Wisdom of the Ages.*

Concept Therapy presents a modern approach to that which the enlightened of all ages must have known. Its job, and one it does so expertly, is to coordinate these truths and to make them more comprehensible. It explains the underlying principle from which all philosophies, religions, and methods of healing spring.

What makes Concept Therapy different from religions,

other philosophies, and from conventional psychological approaches? One of the reasons is that it teaches *the Laws*. The next chapter identifies and explains them. Take heed and don't pass over it lightly. There's a gold mine of exact knowledge for those who have the eyes to see it.

# CHAPTER THREE

## The Laws

"We have a physical body and it is governed by four laws." This was Dr. Fleet speaking at what he calls a "Jam Session." Sometimes prepared, sometimes extemporaneous, these talks are given on an unscheduled basis by himself, one of his instructors, or often an advanced student visiting the Texas ranch which serves as headquarters for the Concept Therapy Institute.

Always there is an air of eager anticipation when it is learned Dr. Fleet will be the speaker. And always a capacity throng fills Taggart Hall, the remodeled army mess building serving as the main assembly room for the institute. No seat is vacant and standing room is at a minimum. Fleet starts his talk at exactly 8:00 P.M. and finishes his last word at ten minutes before nine.

"One of the four laws that govern the body is nourishment," Dr. Fleet explains from the platform. "There is a right way to nourish your body and we teach you that way in Concept Therapy." Everyone present was acquainted with the laws of the body. Besides nourishment there is movement, recuperation and sanitation. It is all fully explained in Fleet's book, *Rays of the Dawn*, published by the Concept Therapy Institute.

All present that evening had read and reread the slim, blue-covered volume. It contained much food for thought, sometimes too much at first. After a student completes his initial Concept Therapy class, he is given the book and it is expected that he will study it. Most do, at least the serious students of the work gladly comply with the request.

Fleet, oblivious to the fact that he was covering familiar ground, went on explaining the basics. His audience gave him the same close attention that they had given at their first exposure to the laws. These people had discovered that a bit more light was shed with each explanation, "new brain cells of recognition were being created," so to speak. It was the fifth or sixth time around, in my case, when the enormity of the proposition finally dawned on me; work with the laws and you change your life.

"We also have twelve laws of the mind," he said, pointing to a large chart that contained the following:

If You Are<br>
OFF THE BEAM<br>
You Will Have Disease

1. INCORRECTLY COMBINED MEALS
2. IMPROPER MUSCULAR EXERCISE
3. IMPROPER RECUPERATION
4. IMPROPER EXTERNAL AND INTERNAL SANITATION
5. FEAR
6. WORRY
7. SELFISHNESS
8. VANITY
9. ANGER
10. CRITICISM
11. ENVY
12. GREED
13. HYPOCRISY
14. PREJUDICE
15. JEALOUSY
16. HATE

These laws constitute the negative expression of the Soul through the senses. The emotions on the chart (5 through 16) are destructive and harmful not only to the person expressing them but to others at whom they are directed. Yet we use them all the time, not realizing it's the same as pointing a loaded gun at ourselves or others and pulling the trigger indiscriminately. When some crisis occurs, the person who at once becomes fearful, "scared to death" of what's going to happen instead of conjuring up strong faith, is expressing negative energy. Likewise when one engages in constant worry over a condition instead of having hope, he is doing untold damage.

"We do have a choice how we express ourselves in any given situation," Fleet often says. "Trouble is, most people just don't know what they bring into their lives when they choose the wrong way to express. Since you got to do something when misfortune comes, choose to operate through the Laws of the Soul and before long you'll change pain into pleasure." He indicated that attention should be focused on the right side of him where he pointed to another chart.

If You Are
ON THE BEAM
You Will Have Health

1. CORRECTLY BALANCED MEALS
2. PROPER MUSCULAR EXERCISE
3. PROPER RECUPERATION
4. EXTERNAL AND INTERNAL SANITATION
5. FAITH
6. HOPE
7. GENEROSITY-CHARITY
8. ASPIRATION
9. PATIENCE
10. SYMPATHY
11. NONINTERFERENCE
12. KINDNESS

13. COURAGE
14. FORGIVENESS
15. DUTY
16. LOVE

"These twelve laws of the Soul," continued Fleet, "constitute the positive expression of the Soul through the senses and are very beneficial and helpful."

I have these two charts hanging in my home. They remind me that I have a choice; that I can choose to have patience instead of anger or sympathy instead of criticism. This is a very direct way of choosing good health instead of illness. Besides the laws of the body, mind, and Soul, Concept Therapy teaches the seven subsidiary Universal Laws (which dovetail and correspond with each other) under the one great Law "God Is" or "Energy Is." Says Fleet, "Upon these Laws all physical Life is based."

Before continuing with an account of what took place that evening, I think it is time we explain these laws in some detail. First, THE LAW OF PERPETUAL TRANSMUTATION OF RADIANT ENERGY: This law explains the truth that everything in the material universe, all that we see, hear, touch, taste, or smell, our emotions and our thoughts are simply manifestations of energy.

Those specializing in the field of physics tell us science has learned that we can't create energy or destroy energy, just change it. In fact, we do that particular act every day of our lives. The food we eat is not destroyed, merely transmuted into fuel for our body. Another example is boiling water changing into steam. The elements of the water haven't been destroyed, just transmuted into a gaseous form.

If science admits that everything is energy (perhaps I'm offending some "purists" by using such a generality, but I'm sure the lay reader prefers me to keep it simple and not obscure the truth by a needless adherence to strict scientific terminology) then that means our problems, too, are just energy. If we can change energy at will by applying the proper methods, as we transmute water into gas by means of heat, so too can we change the energy we dubbed a problem into the energy known as a solution by the energy of understanding. This law gives you a basis from which to work.

Second comes THE LAW OF RELATIVITY: Under this law we find that all things are relative. The laws of the little are the laws of the great. By use of this law one is able to overcome the pains of life, and build a "Heaven on Earth." We'll spend more time explaining the use of this law in Chapter Four.

Next comes THE LAW OF VIBRATION: This law embodies the fact that all things are in motion. All things vibrate; nothing rests. The uninformed touch a table and say, "Surely this is not moving. It feels solid and looks very stationary to me." The man of science knows better. The table to him is a group of whirling electrons filled with energy, each electron keeping in its orbit and never getting out of its assigned place.

The solidness of any object is just an illusion of the senses. The scientist knows that if he would measure the distance between any two electrons in the table, he would get a distance that is proportionately greater than the actual material distance between Europe and America. In his masterful work, *Phase Three of Conceptology*, Fleet asserts that vibration can be transmitted from one object to another or from one human to another, through the medium of the electron. "Vibratory control of the body, mind, or Soul of a person for the restoration of human equilibrium of health is possible," he claims. "It may be exercised through the medium of the resonant electric waves of the brain cells, passing from doctor to patient or parent to child. This process becomes understood when the Law of Vibration we teach in our classes is fully visualized."

The fourth law taught is THE LAW OF POLARITY: Under this law we see that all opposites are identical in nature and differ only in degree. Everything in the universe has its

36

pair of opposites. Understanding this law enables one to free himself from the effects of sorrow, sickness, worry, fear, and all the other negative expressions of life.

For instance, a man living in the arid Southwest would say, "Water is good, in fact it's like gold out here." And we all, of course, agree. But the victim of a flood would say, "Rampaging water has inundated my land, wrecked my house, and left me penniless. It's bad." Water, like everything else, has the potential to be either good or bad for us. This law helps you to see a thing as it really is; an important prerequisite in controlling your life.

Now comes THE LAW OF RHYTHM: This law explains that everything in the universe is in rhythm, moving to and fro, in and out as the seasons, the tides, and even the negative and positive expressions of our thoughts as well as the rhythmic swing of consciousness and unconsciousness. Do you ever wonder why sometimes you're apt to be moody, resentful, and perhaps fly off the handle while on other occasions you take things in stride, are more forgiving and perhaps even joyous, although nothing is changed? It is explained by the Law of Rhythm.

By understanding how the negative swing of the pendulum will incline us toward uncomfortable feelings and a less than desirable disposition, we become able to guard against giving vent to outbursts of fear, worry, selfishness, greed, jealousy, or hatred. Fleet writes, "When negative energy surges through us striving for expression and we refrain from expressing it, the pendulum will swing back to the positive much faster if the negative has not found an outlet."

Sigmund Freud, in 1910, confided to Ernest Jones, "I could not contemplate with any sort of comfort a life without work. Creative imagination and work go together with me; I take no delight in anything else. That would be a prescription for happiness were it not for the terrible thought that one's productivity depended on sensitive moods. What is one to do on a day when thoughts cease to flow and the proper words won't come?"

If Dr. Freud knew the workings of the Law of Rhythm he might have saved himself much grief on those "down days." He would know exactly what to do and more important what not to do. Unfortunately he did not know, just as millions of others do not, and as a result they engage in acts that bring much remorse as soon as the pendulum swings back to the positive.

THE LAW OF CAUSE AND EFFECT shows that there is no such thing as chance. Every cause has its effect; every effect, its cause. The Hindus use the word "Karma" to represent this law. Another term might be "reward and punishment." The Bible makes reference to it with the statement: "Be not deceived; God is not mocked: for whatsoever a man soweth, that shall he also reap."

"Choosing is another word for sowing," writes Fleet in his *Phase Three* text. "As you choose, so shall you get." Farmers know this law as it applies to the sowing of seed. If they sow corn they do not expect wheat; they will always get corn. The law is the same for the physical, mental, and spiritual planes as well. By selecting the right foods and health habits and those physical things which are conducive to peace, you will reap peace. That's just common sense.

The same goes for the mental plane. If you're the type that "flies off the handle" because some unthinking motorist cuts in front of you or beats you to a parking place you had mentally reserved for yourself, if you react with revenge at some real or fancied slight, if instead of generosity you respond to life with greed, be assured that you are planting a crop of negative effects and sooner or later you will have to harvest it.

We've touched on the physical and mental planes so far as the Law of Cause and Effect is concerned, but there is also the spiritual sphere to be considered. Concept Therapy believes strongly in dealing with all three planes. The spiritual

38

plane concerns a person's ACTS. Dr. Fleet teaches, "Whenever choosing an act, one should determine carefully if it is wrong action or right action."

Some years ago, I was the radio and TV director in charge of writing and producing all the radio and television commercials for a Los Angeles advertising agency. It was a medium-sized outfit and one that required all its personnel to "wear many hats." Besides all my other responsibilities, I was Master of Ceremonies on a weekly hour TV show.

In the midst of my busy schedule, I received a letter marked "urgent." It was not too unlike other letters I had received in the past. "You don't know me but a mutual friend suggested that I contact you," it read, "I wonder if you could help get me a job out there. Our doctor said California would have the best climate for my child." It seems the letter writer had a good advertising position in Chicago but because of health reasons he had to move his family to the West.

The same day the letter arrived, yet another work burden was placed on my shoulders. I was given the responsibility for all broadcast media selection. That meant I had to decide on what radio stations throughout the United States and Canada I would buy the time to run commercials I had created for our most important client, a foreign car firm. Hundreds of thousands of dollars were involved. My decisions had to be correct and, as you can imagine, I was literally swamped with all kinds of detail work. My time was necessarily limited to only the most important business.

After hurriedly reading the letter with some annoyance at this untimely intrusion, I crumpled it and was about to throw it in the wastepaper basket when a second thought made me pause. At that instant I consciously chose to sow compassion instead of my usual callowness. I spent half an hour composing an answer and trying to be as truthful as possible. I couldn't help him get another job but I cited my own experience. I had come to California without friends or business connections and had "made it." Anything is possible and well worth the try, I wrote.

The letter was promptly mailed and forgotten in the pressure cooker that is the advertising business. A year and a half later, when I had my fill of the long hours, the constant intrigue and instability of my occupation, and had handed in my resignation without another job in sight, something happened. You might term it coincidence. I say it was cause and effect, the law in action.

One of CBS Radio's talented on-the-air personalities, Bob Grant, a long-time friend from Chicago, telephoned me. "Bill, I know you've got a pretty good deal at the agency you're with and I'm not sure you'd even be interested, but I felt inclined to call you and let you know about a writing job that just opened up over here at CBS." I thanked Bob and told him I was very much interested indeed.

I arranged for an appointment and the following day I was interviewed. The man doing the hiring, the one in need of a writer, was the same person who eighteen months previously had sent me a letter asking for help. Later I learned he had written almost a dozen other letters and I had been the only one to take time to answer him. I was signed to a contract and it turned out to be the best position I had ever had up to then. Truly, I had reaped a rich harvest.

Lastly, is THE LAW OF GENDER: This law holds that behind all creation, whether physical, mental, or spiritual there must be the masculine and feminine principle. It is the action of the male principle upon the female principle that gives rise to all creation.

"Actually the word creation is incorrect. Nothing is ever created in that it is made of nothing," Fleet stresses. "All things are merely the changing of something that was into something that now is. The Law of Gender on a purely physical plane manifests itself as sex."

Concept Therapy establishes that the Law of Gender holds true in the mental realm as well as the physical realm. The masculine principle is the Originative factor. It acts upon the feminine principle or receptive and Executive factor. Just as with the physical realm a period of incubation is required before an offspring is produced directly from the Executive, formative member. "I can see this pretty clearly in biology," an industrialist told Fleet, "but how does it affect, say, business?" The answer was, of course, obvious. "In your business as in every other business," Fleet replied, "it is the action of the originative capital upon the receptive and executive labor that gives rise to the commercial product . . . the product springing, after its period of formation, directly from the executive member."

"O.K.," retorted Mr. Industrialist, "I get that picture, but now in the mental realm it's still kind of obscure to me." To clarify the law, Fleet explained, "We have a dual mind, the conscious and that great area known as the subconscious. We have been taught that the conscious mind possesses the Power to Originate trains of causation; therefore it would be safe in naming it the male Principle of the mind."

"I get it," our businessman friend said. "That would be the Originative Factor." Fleet, very pleased, agreed and said, "The subconscious is inert and dormant, insofar as causes are concerned, until it has been impregnated with an idea, such an idea always originating in the conscious. Therefore, the subconscious may properly be referred to as the Female Principle, the part which, once having been given the necessary premise or idea, proceeds to Execute It."

In the light of this information, it is clear to see that you should be very careful in what ideas you select. I mean ideas such as failure or sickness or any of the other negative ones. Because if they become injected into the subconscious, you can be sure that after a period of incubation, they will be born in your body or your life. In following chapters this will be made even clearer to you.

As is often pointed out in official Concept Therapy literature and lecture platforms all over the United States and

Canada, these laws are not original with Concept Therapy. They are an adaptation of principles which have been taught down through the ages. Concept Therapy presents them from a new approach so that they may be better understood and more easily applied in one's life. Without proper knowledge it is almost impossible to take full advantage of the power for good that is inherent within them. When one is able to, it means living in harmony with the universe. Needless to say, this is a goal worth striving for.

CHAPTER FOUR

## Relatively Speaking

In the previous chapter we started by describing a "Jam Session" over which Dr. Fleet presided. On this particular Texas evening, he wanted to clarify just how the Law of Relativity can be used in solving human equilibrium problems. "Everything we can know is related in some way to another thing," Fleet explained.

He, of course, wasn't referring to Mr. Einstein's law, which he said deals only with matter, but with the ancient Hermetic law that deals with the relation between things of the physical plane, the thoughts we think, and the acts that we perform. By now it should be clear that these laws are a perspective-giving device. They enable you to see a thing, thought, or a situation as it really is and not as it appears to be from some prejudiced viewpoint.

I once heard an exponent of the controversial psychedelic drugs argue the case for LSD. He described what he believed to be its great value by claiming it added to a person's insight. "It's as if," he said, "any model you have of the universe is based on a fixed relationship between an incoming nerve fiber and an outgoing nerve fiber. When you chemically alter the situation an incoming nerve fiber may activate many outgoing fibers. That would give you much richer data than you had before when dealing with any concept."

Many psychiatrists seriously researching LSD fail to be convinced as yet that a dose of it will bring extra maturity and an all-seeing, all-knowing enlightenment from the mind's critical faculty. They do know of its hallucinatory effect, though. But the LSD proponent I was referring to spoke of a many-leveled perception state of consciousness in which it would be difficult to keep any stereotype of the fixed pattern which would be your old personality, the person you were before taking the drug.

One of the many advantages of the awareness gained through Concept Therapy instruction over drug induced "instant wisdom" is the small risk of losing your identity in an artificially caused frightening flash (an experience that drives some to suicide). But more important, I believe, is the fact that you don't hammer into your subconscious a dynamic and self-defeating suggestion that says in effect: With my own moral ability I am unable to accomplish needed emotional and spiritual growth without the aid of a prop."

In a concerted effort to keep people from thinking of Concept Therapy as a religion, Dr. Fleet resorts to some pretty bizarre acts. Mottos, attractively framed and neatly hung in eye-catching locations, adorn the Concept Therapy Institute. Signs such as:

"EACH DOG TO HIS OWN VOMIT.
EACH PIG TO HIS OWN SLOP."

Ed Wagoner, who along with his wife Mary is in charge of tape recording special lectures for the Institute, was visibly shocked when he first encountered the above statement. After recovering from the surprise, it didn't take him long to sense a deeper significance in the message. At the first opportunity, he questioned Dr. Fleet about its meaning.

"After we instruct a person in our classes and he refuses to utilize what he has learned; for some psychological reason he doesn't heal himself or reverse his misfortune, then we don't interfere with his personal choice. We say he is welcome to his vomit or slop. We don't impose our truth on him," was Dr. Fleet's candid reply.

His philosophy teaches that most illness is caused by faulty reasoning of the originative factor of personality. It is this part of us that thinks disease and therefore causes the Soul to act itself into disease. The conscious can think and cause acts that go contrary to the great power within. Food faddism is a perfect example. Understand, I am not "knocking" healthy foods or a balanced diet. I love vegetables and fruits and at least three times a week my dinner consists of huge salads and natural cheeses. Proper nutrition is a part of the Concept Therapy philosophy. What I'm referring to is, "health-food enslavement."

In his excellent book, *Man's Presumptuous Brain*, A. T. W. Simeons, M.D., writes: "The simple end products of normal digestion are always the same, regardless of the form in which protein, fat, sugar, or starch is eaten. The form in which food is eaten makes very little difference to the inner chemistry of the body. That is why the countless and often contradictory dietary taboos that abound throughout the world have little or no physiological foundation, however much their advocates may cherish them."

Some people would swear on a Bible that chili, beans, and hot pepper will kill you. Yet, there are remarkably healthy individuals who subside on just that diet with little evidence that it is detrimental for them to eat this kind of food. Consider the Eskimo who fares very well eating fish and blubber. But imagine, suggests Dr. Simeons, what would happen if he were suddenly yanked out of his environment and placed in a land where the diet was predominantly milk, rice, and hot pickles. Digestively speaking he would not be any worse off after a day or two, provided his mental likes and dislikes, his superstitions and his fears could be controlled.

When the above theory was presented and followed up with medical proof, it caused quite a stir in scientific and lay circles, yet Concept Therapy has taught just this for over thirty years.

The Law of Gender and the principle of the Composite Personality clearly explain how certain good and healthy foods can produce disorders in the body because of "fantasies born of uncritical self-observation and the cortical habit of jumping quickly to conclusions, however scientifically implausible."

But now back to Taggart Hall and to the man on the platform. "I want to tell you a true story. This really happened to me." With these words Dr. Fleet launched into a tale that beautifully illustrated the point he was trying to make. This technique of teaching was his favorite and one he used often and with great skill. I remember the story well.

Once when he was a practicing chiropractor in San Antonio, a lady came to his office. She was whining and full of self-pity. "Doctor," she cried, "you have got to do something for me. I feel lower than a snake's belly. I've got the 'miseries.' I feel like I am the sickest patient you ever had."

Dr. Fleet, commiserating with her, said, "Sounds like you really are in bad shape. Step over to this blackboard." Startled, she asked, "What's the blackboard got to do with helping me?" Dr. Fleet just handed her a piece of chalk and continued with his plan. Taking up another piece of chalk he drew a medial line and labeled one side health and the other side disease.

HEALTH_____DISEASE

"Now, Mrs. M, show me where you think you are on the line." Unhesitatingly, she placed herself right up to the DISEASE part of the line.

HEALTH_____(M) DISEASE

"I'm absolutely the sickest person alive, Dr. Fleet," she said as her eyes welled with tears. Fleet sympathetically handed her a tissue but didn't stop.

"I want you to look at this group of case histories for a minute or two, Mrs. M." Before she could protest he handed her an eight-by-ten file card with the heading CANCER.

"Here's a poor soul with cancer of the face. Will you just look at that pathetic picture."

His patient gasped. The sight horrified her. Innocently, Dr. Fleet inquired, "Where do you think this person should be on our line?" Without a word she erased the line representing her proximity to the word disease and placed the cancer victim there. She then drew another line behind the one with the cancer condition. "I still feel pretty bad but I'm certainly not as bad as what you just showed me."

Dr. Fleet handed her a second card. Timidly, the lady took it in her trembling hands and obligingly read what was on it, unsuccessfully trying to avoid seeing the accompanying photograph. It was a quadruple amputee; often referred to as a "basketcase." Letting a few minutes pass in silence the doctor then said, "Considering that this man is completely helpless, not even able to shave himself, comb his hair, or feed himself, where does he go on our line?"

"Down here, he's really bad off. It's . . . it's just terrible. What, I mean, how did it happen?"

"An automobile accident. Now, Mrs. M., where do we put you?" She stared at the blackboard with the chalk lines and then thoughtfully said, "Up here closer toward . . . health."

HEALTH_____(M) (C) (A) DISEASE

Next, Fleet handed her a card concerning an arthritis case and the process was the same. Always the lady being truthful had to move herself closer and closer to the health aspect of human equilibrium. In relation to the others who were sick, Mrs. M. was obviously healthier. Finally, after a couple of other potent examples, she put herself over the line on the health side. "My God, when I came in I thought I was sick, but I know now I'm lucky to be like I am. I feel much better." Out she flew, not even looking back.

The possibilities to test this law are unlimited. For instance, let us concern ourselves with the subject of money.

We all agree that what to one man is being well off, to

47

another could be the edge of poverty. It is all relative. (There's that word again.) Let's see if it really is true. We visit "skid row," the poorest section of the city. We approach an inhabitant of the slum area and ask him how he's doing. "Great! I just got a swell job after almost six weeks' layoff," he answers. "I'm making fifty dollars a week. Boy! Will my wife and kids be happy."

But wait. Another citizen we questioned in a middle-class neighborhood complained bitterly about his salary. "A hundred dollars a week is just not enough." Yet in relation to the "skid row" man, this fellow was truly affluent, making twice as much per week and living in a finer part of town with more opportunity for a better life. The inescapable conclusion is that money in itself is not the criterion that signifies wealth or poverty but rather it is the attitude of the two individuals concerned.

The argument I usually get at this point is exemplified best by the remark tossed at me by a young businessman who, after listening to my explanation, said, "Sounds like you're just making a fancy excuse for failure." Yet he was as concerned as I was about the mental attitude held by a mutual friend and what it was doing to him internally.

The executive in question was bemoaning the fact that he had just lost over twenty-five thousand dollars in an unsuccessful business venture. Almost all of his entire life's savings had gone down the drain. True, he still had a fine position with an advertising agency. He owned his own home and his mortgage payments and upkeep were far from excessive. He even had two cars and a paid-up life insurance policy, yet he was desolate because of his enormous financial loss.

There are a lot of people who would like to be in his financial shoes, the investment failure notwithstanding. His salary totals over five hundred dollars a week and at the end of the year he can expect a large cash bonus. But when I tried to comfort him by pointing out the positive aspects of his situation he snarled, "Don't keep telling me what I've got.

Look at what I've lost." He'll lose a lot more if he continues his present line of thinking.

The point I am getting at is that unless you do something to halt the morbid thought energy that in turn churns up your innards, you will be the recipient of some very real and dangerous physical problems. I refer you back to the preceding chapter. A number of authorities with impressive scientific credentials have gone on record to sound the alarm that thoughts *can* kill.

Am I being overly sensational? Remember what Dr. Rangell reported about bacteria finding it easier to infest people who are emotionally irritated. Also, recall the fact that many medical men say that appendicitis can be brought on by emotional upset. Keep in mind that bodily changes occur because emotion is supposed to cause motion. Fear, for example, in the cave man, prepared him for fight or flight.

"So what if I am scared of losing my job," I snapped, "long as they don't find out at work, I'm still holding my own." That was my attitude during my first Concept Therapy class. I was explaining my feelings to Rev. Crump during one of the breaks. "Sure I'm afraid, but so what?" Like so many others I figured being fearful didn't amount to much, just as long as nobody found out. The awakening was rude.

"Know what happens inside you when you get afraid, Bill?" the Concept Therapy instructor asked. "How should I know, I'm no sawbones," came back my answer. Ever on the defensive, my words came out harsher than I really wanted. Rev. Crump was unperturbed. He had met my type before.

"Fear, for example, tenses you up. Your body responds by certain physiological and chemical changes that take place. Adrenalin is released which causes the heart to beat more rapidly. The muscles of the stomach and intestines contract, forcing the blood out into general circulation, increasing the rate of breathing, and causing other changes meant to gear the body for action," he informed me.

I forced a weak smile and said, "Look! When I'm afraid

I don't do anything physical. Certainly I don't run and I'm not about to slug my boss no matter how obnoxious he is." Looking at me square in the eyes, his gaze not wavering one bit, Rev. Crump made a verbal thrust that sunk deep. "Exactly, Bill. And these powerful, continuing emotional disturbances like fear and jealousy (I had that, too, as well as envy, hate, worry, and anger) can seriously affect the working of the body organs."

He was speaking the truth. My physical condition attested to the validity of his words. Almost everyone is aware that at least 50 per cent (if not more) of all people seeking medical attention today are suffering from ailments brought on or made worse by such emotional factors as prolonged worry, anxiety, or fear. "Emotional tensions often play a prominent role in certain kinds of heart and circulatory disorders, especially high blood pressure, digestive ailments, such as, peptic ulcer and colitis, headache and joint and muscular pains, skin disorders, and some allergies." So say psychological experts employed by the Metropolitan Life Insurance Company in their excellent booklet, *Emotions and Physical Health*.

The point is, and please forgive me for being somewhat redundant, we must learn to do something *logical* (remember that key word) if we are to avoid triggering the aforementioned disturbances that do such dreadful damage to us. Alright, so you concede the point, we must do something; but what? One thing, it's for sure that someone telling you not to be fearful, worried, or angry is a pure waste of time. It's utter nonsense to imagine that kind of advice will or could ever be heeded.

Of what value is it once you have leaped out of an airplane high in the sky, *sans* parachute, for me to shout, "Don't hit the ground too hard or you'll get hurt." No matter how valid the message, once you have jumped you are in the grip of gravity's law and despite the most fervent wishes, desires, or beliefs to the contrary, an awful splash is going to be made when you reach the earth.

I'm reminded of the story concerning the positive thinker who fell out of a ninety-fifth-story window of the Empire State building in New York City. All the way down as he passed each floor on his speedy descent, he would smile and say, "Well, I haven't hit bottom yet." I wonder if this is not indeed what a good many professed positive-thinkers and "mental-science religionists" are actually doing. "By their fruits shall ye know them" is still the best gauge to determine if a person "walks like he talks." If your present way of life, your philosophy or beliefs have not completely satisfied your inner and outer needs, perhaps Concept Theory can.

From Freud, "the father of psychoanalysis," we learn the severe consequences of repression. On the other hand, if in deciding not to repress our emotions we haul off and punch our antagonist in the nose, we will quickly become familiar with the penalty civil law imposes on us for antisocial acts. Husbands and wives subscribing to the policy that it is far better to express one's inner thoughts no matter how illicit the desire or hostile the action rather than chance the ill effects of repression, crowd our divorce courts daily.

Well, then, are we doomed no matter what choice we make? Is there no way to escape this vicious circle of being damned if we don't and damned if we do? By this time I am sure that my answer will not in the least surprise you. Concept Therapy offers a proven, usable way to "break the connection" between you and the "buttons" others can and do push that cause you to respond in an emotionally destructive way.

# CHAPTER FIVE

# The Mind: Trick or Treat

Although I have covered Relativity pretty thoroughly in the preceding chapter, I came across something in a 1965 issue of *TV GUIDE* that is just too good not to include. It illustrates once again how our mind can trick us. It can make us see something that isn't there and just as easily prevent us from observing the obvious.

Melvin Durslag, writing about TV actor and former big-league baseball player Chuck Connors, quotes the star of the *Rifleman, Branded,* and the *Arrest and Trial* television series as saying, "I am anything but well-heeled." For the uninformed, the term "well-heeled" (in the parlance of the street) means being rich, having a lot of money, enjoying the many luxuries of life.

What amount of money do you think one must have to consider himself rich? When he was a youngster in Brooklyn, growing up in a $30-a-month, cold-water flat, I'm sure if someone told Mr. Connors that someday he would own a $100,000 cantilever-design home in the Hollywood Hills and, by his own admission, be worth a quarter of a million dollars, he would most certainly admit that if this ever happened he would indeed consider himself "well-heeled." Yet, today he really believes he is not. Why?

The mind to most is a deep mystery and well it should be.

Concept Therapy unveils the truth as to what actually constitutes the mind (that's just a name that describes the activity of the cells of the brain) and delves in depth on how the personality functions. It familiarizes its students with the seemingly paradoxical machinations of the mental processes in the lessons on the Mind, Factors of Personality, Composite Personality, the Basic Concept, the Becoming of the Faculties, and Laws Governing the change of Concepts.

"Don't let your mind trick you," Dr. Fleet often cautions. "People see what they 'need' to see," say psychologist Gary Steiner and sociologist Bernard Berelson in their noteworthy book, *Human Behavior: An Inventory of Scientific Findings.* "The pupil of the eye dilates on seeing pleasant things and contracts at unpleasant sights. Coins of the exact same size look bigger to poor children than to rich children."

"Modern-day man," conclude Steiner and Berelson, "has a vast talent for distorting reality because of psychological needs. For the most part "he thinks what fits his wishes, says what pleases his peers, avoids conflicts, and protects his neuroses. He votes with his friends, wants what he has to work for, and thinks that his group or organization ranks higher than it does. If threatened with disillusionment, he simply slides into fantasy and reality pays the price."

But what is reality? Is it worth discovering? Frankly, facts do have a way of seeming unfriendly. Perhaps that is why we allow ourselves to be surrounded on all sides by sham and pretense. Why should we break down the walls of our artificial milieu, anyway? "Know the truth and the truth shall make you free," we are told. But do we believe this?

Our brains are jammed full of fantasies and unproven theories we label as facts. So many of our concepts, those that we hold so dear, are utterly false and yet they influence us more than we are willing to admit; more than we are able to understand. Certain foods are *bad* for us. Certain foods are *good* for us. We *can* do that and we are unable to do this. What is true; what is false?

In *Phase One*, Dr. Fleet writes, "Men have divided that which they call the mind into many different parts, but there are two portions with which everyone is more or less familiar; namely, the conscious and subconscious." The conscious can also be called the objective or educated part of the mind (also the originative member) while the subconscious can be called the subjective, innate (or executive) part.

In Concept Therapy much is made over the fact that the conscious mind reasons in two ways: Inductively and deductively, but the subconscious reasons only deductively. It is pertinent to our thesis that we examine these diametrically opposite forms of reason. You will shortly discover the bearing this knowledge has in explaining how we can change, if we so desire, our present predicament and shape the future to our liking. It will also aid us in clearing away from our thinking the clouds of confusion.

Deductive reasoning is where the conclusion necessarily follows from the premises, so that, if the premises are true, the conclusion must be true. In the time of Christopher Columbus, the reigning premise, certainly of the Christian world, was that everything in the Holy Bible was *literal* truth. When simple sailors of that era heard their priests quote *Revelations* 7.1: "After this I saw four angels standing at the four corners of the earth holding back the four winds of the earth that no winds might blow on earth or sea or against any tree," they naturally jumped to the conclusion that the earth was flat.

This erroneous belief was a common conclusion, and although false, nevertheless exerted strong influence on the thinking of kings as well as commoners. Merchant seamen refused to venture far from the sight of shore, lest their ships topple over the edge of the earth and fall into the bottomless abyss. On the other hand the Vikings, lacking Christian indoctrination and therefore ignorant about the "fact" of the four angels on each corner of the earth, were uninhibited and merrily sailed across vast oceans and discovered new continents because of their "ignorance." It took brave men to dare to reason inductively in those days. Even now, in this enlightened age of ours, it is no mean feat.

Consider the courage of Galileo Galilei in the Sixteenth Century. Because he was the rarest of all species, an *original thinker*, he could not, he would not, accept something as factual just because it had been decreed a fact by those in the seat of power. He risked his life to challenge authority based on age and prestige. He set out to prove Aristotle, the greatest of the Greek philosophers, wrong.

It had been believed for 2,000 years that a heavy object fell faster than a light one. If it was twice as heavy, it naturally fell twice as fast. Who said so? Why, no less an authority than the great Aristotle. For twenty centuries mankind had blindly, without questioning, accepted his word on the matter.

Then one fine day, legend has it, Galileo lugged two different-sized cannon balls up the winding staircase to the top of the leaning tower of Pisa. He carefully let them both fall at the same time. The most educated men of his day were shocked when he dropped those two cannon balls—a heavy one and a lighter one. Actually they were doubly surprised. First, to think that someone had the audacity to question Aristotle; and second, to discover that *both* cannonballs hit the ground at the same time.

What Galileo demonstrated was a new problem-solving method, based not on authority of age and prestige but rather on the authority of observation and experiment, as Wendell Johnson pointed out. Columbus, too, ignored what others believed (feared) and forged ahead following in the footsteps of the few brave and thoughtful souls who insisted on utilizing to the utmost their God-given power to reason inductively, as well as deductively. The ability to reason properly separates the great from the lowly. "Inductive reasoning is the process of reasoning from the part to the whole, from the specific to the general; that is, one must gather a group of facts and reason from them to a general idea."

In his *Phase One* text, Dr. Fleet explains that the two forms of reasoning can be likened to what takes place at a court trial. I believe it's an ingenious analogy. "The prosecutor uses inductive reasoning. He gathers a group of facts and reasons therefrom that the accused is guilty, whereas the defense always uses deductive reasoning. He begins with the idea that his client is not guilty and then assembles the facts to prove his ideas."

He goes on to explain that it is the same with the executive factor of the personality or the subconscious powerhouse within, sometimes referred to as the Spirit. "When IT has been provided with an idea—good, bad or indifferent—it proceeds to prove or carry out that idea to its most rigorously logical conclusion." I'm reminded of an amusing hypnosis demonstration I viewed in a Hollywood nightclub. The stage hypnotist gave the suggestion to a willing subject that he was a great opera star. Then the command to sing was given.

With complete confidence and great aplomb, the man started to sing. It was, I recall, an aria from *Carmen* complete with broad and dramatic gestures. His wife was somewhat astonished at her husband's rather good performance. Afterwards, when she stepped up to the stage to retrieve her spouse, she readily admitted to the audience that her husband ordinarily never sang anything in his waking state, not even in the shower. She was completely mystified.

Hypnosis for the most part is nothing to laugh at or treat lightly. I concur with those who advocate caution where hypnosis is concerned, but I most certainly do not believe it should be a monopoly to the medicos. After all, they (the medical doctors and scientists) scoffed at its validity and actually tried to squelch continuing investigation of this phenomenon. Only until recent times has hypnosis been accepted by some M.D.'s and psychiatrists. It was the stage hypnotists and unorthodox healers who promulgated the so-called "black art" and kept it alive for humanity to rediscover.

When Dr. Fleet introduced comprehensive hypnosis instruction to emphasize the Principle of the Composite Personality and the Law of Gender, half of the entire Concept Therapy organization severed all ties with the institute. These people were afraid; ignorance often causes fright, and they wanted no part of any group that delved into such dangerous and "unchristian" practices. Several Concept Therapy instructors felt the entire movement would collapse and begged Dr. Fleet to abandon the study of hypnosis. He naturally refused to retreat a step.

It is my personal opinion that only in *Phase One* of Conceptology can one really understand the value of what is called hypnotism. It's interesting to note that a British surgeon, James Braid, was responsible for the name hypnotism. Prior to 1942, the hypnotic state was referred to as Mesmerism. Braid thought he was inducing a state of sleep so he drew on the Greek word "Hypnos" meaning sleep.

After further experience with hypnosis he discovered to his chagrin that what he assumed to be a true sleep was actually not. It was, he finally observed, a concentration of the mind. Being an honest man and a dedicated researcher, he was determined to set the record straight and so he attempted to change hypnosis to mono-ideaism, but by that time the words *hypnosis* and *hypnotism* were deeply rooted in almost every language. He had to give up trying to change the name and this misnomer has never ceased causing untold confusion.

This concentration of the mind, what does it mean anyway? Why is it so important and what can it do? The late Arden R. Hedge, M.D., a past president of the American Institute of Hypnosis, in an article in the first issue of the *Journal of the American Institute of Hypnosis* wrote, "We have within us far greater powers or capabilities to help ourselves physically than we formerly believed possible. Thus through greater control at the subconscious level, we are better equipped to alter, for beneficial purposes, our circulation, metabolism, digestion, and a long list of other vital functions. Even EKG's (Electrocardiograms) can be changed, antibody counts increased, and allergies eradicated."

Also, in the April, 1963 issue of that same publication, W. Grenville Riddell, M.D., wrote that the hypnotic—mind over matter—positive thinking, suggestion training he had received had proved invaluable. "Not only in treating casually emotionally disturbed patients but in obesity control, asthma, allergic dermatitis and urticaria; nervous dyspepsia 'butterflies,' nervous colitis and diarrhea, apprehensive post coronary cases, marital disruption cases that need calming and reassurance, enuresis, frigidity, emergency accidents of fractures, and wounds that require hypno-anaesthesia to correct or suture; training for pelvic anaesthesia for delivery, or first trimester calmative correction of the usual nausea and vomiting of psychosomatic origin. All these, and many other varied conditions encountered in one's everyday general practice, respond well to hypnotism. It is especially useful in general surgery for the pre and post operative patient benefit, and promotes the doctor's own satisfaction in rapid recovery."

That's a mouthful. Is he referring to some "miracle" drug? Black Magic? A secret formula? No, he is just enumerating some of the amazing benefits that can come about through suggestion. Yes, I said suggestion. For what else is hypnosis, if not an example of the astounding power of suggestion? Richard R. Parlour, M.D., a psychiatrist, defines hypnosis as an altered state of consciousness in which the patient's mind is concentrated on certain things *suggested* by the hypnotist so that most other incoming stimuli are ignored.

It is the particular suggestion that determines the manifestation of certain bodily functions. Increased susceptibility to suggestion is a vital cog in the phenomenon of hypnosis. Both the conscious and the subconscious mind is subject to influence and direction, but it has been discovered that when a thought is lodged in the latter it is more amenable to external control, more influential than when it simply holds a place in the conscious.

Someone might tell you that it is a very hot day when in fact it is not. Further they might suggest to you that the temperature is rising and that you are very, very warm and uncomfortable. You might even consider this a possibility for awhile but your reasoning soon tells you otherwise and you would dismiss the words of your friend as nonsense.

But suppose a skilled hypnotist told you the same thing after securing your agreement to allow yourself to be hypnotized, or perhaps he didn't get your agreement but had secured your undivided attention through direct or indirect fascination; what would be your reaction to the suggestion that it was unseasonably hot? Would you be able to reason otherwise? Could you examine a group of facts and come to the conclusion that the temperature was normal? Would this be possible under hypnosis?

The answer is obvious. The subconscious mind does not reason on the validity of suggestions given to it. Be it good, bad, or indifferent. As was stated before, it immediately carries it out to its most rigorously logical conclusion. In this instance, where you have been told it was a very, very hot day, you would feel uncomfortably warm and probably start to perspire. No doubt you would remove as much of your clothing as dignity permits.

I witnessed a demonstration where the aforementioned suggestion had been given to a hypnotized lady. All present were invited to convince her that it was not hot. We showed her a thermometer but she waved it away saying it was not working properly. Several other thermometers were brought to her and we all swore that it was not overly warm. Then inventing an elaborate excuse, she said, "It's my metabolism, I always feel this warm." Here was a lady who, prior to engaging in the experiment, continually complained of having "thin blood," claiming she froze even in the summer.

The hypnotist, through agreement or fascination, is able to bypass the critical faculty of the subject's consciousness and communicate directly with his subconscious. In auto-suggestion or self-hypnosis, you lodge your own images in your subconscious without interfering doubt-thoughts that question the commands. By the way, one learns quickly in Concept Therapy that a concept, idea, or suggestion must be logical to you before it can lodge in your subconscious.

It is surprising how illogical happiness becomes for so many people. That's why most motivations for wealth, health, companionship, employment, et cetera fail to manifest. Those positive thoughts just rattle around the conscious part of the mind never sinking into the specific factor of personality that carries out the originative orders. A lot of good it is to keep muttering "Divine love protects me. I am a child of God. I am safe always," and then tremble all over and be scared to death as you venture into what you fear to be a dangerous locale.

The subconscious doesn't become impressed with words but rather by feelings. Therefore, when you affirm you are courageous but you feel frightened, guess what message the power within is getting and guess what it will be manifesting in your mind, your body and your life. Many people think a few positive thoughts a day and feel negative a few thousand times an hour. That's taking one step forward and a dozen backwards.

Dr. William S. Kroger is a Los Angeles specialist in psychosomatic illness, as well as an obstetrician and gynecologist. He says, "Hypnosis itself does not cure, but it allows a patient to use his imagination to help. Many times the imagination hinders cure and fights the will to get better. In any contest between the imagination and the will, the imagination will always win. That's why it's important to get the imagination working for a cure."

Have we been overlooking the power of our imagination? Too often, I believe, we downgrade the value of imagination as a resource worth cultivating. Sure, it's fine for writers, actors, or artists, but for everyday living for good health, for bringing to us that which we yearn, how could it help? "Keep your head out of the clouds and your feet firmly on the ground," is the admonition from the "solid" citizen. And the

60

multitude take heed of this advice. The familiar phrase, "It was *just* your imagination, *nothing* really," is mute testimony to where imagination has fallen in the scale of human importance.

Imagination, along with repetition, concentration, and suggestion, is another key to unlock the almost unbelievable power residing, for the most part, untapped within us. The truth is that we all use our imagination unconsciously. When we worry about tomorrow we are imagining something, *feeling* something about an occurrence that has not yet taken place. The future is in our imagination and our imagination shapes the future. *I'm afraid I won't get the job. I don't think I can pass the test. I'm sure I won't find what I want.* Those are all instances of imagining something negatively that hasn't yet taken place. The next chapter explains how to make your imagination work wonders for you and create what you want to have happen in the future.

# CHAPTER SIX

## Image Drama

"Listen, you big ape . . . I have more brains in my little finger than you have in that oversized and underdeveloped head of yours! What's more, I don't need this job; I've got a dozen offers at twice the salary you're paying me. I quit!"

A smile of satisfaction slowly spread over my flushed face as I savoured the virulent verbiage. True, it was a silent dialogue, confined to the innermost recesses of the mind, and although I knew my employer would never hear these thoughts, I did derive a certain amount of relief and pleasure from mentally staging this fantasy.

My thought-words were never destined to make the transmutation from the astral plane to the corporeal; at least not in their original form. Yet, someday, had I continued on with this dangerous little game they would have made their damning presence known to me. A headache, stomach pains, perhaps an ulcer, not to mention the prospect of a new job with another "villainous" employer would most certainly be my reward for such mental activity.

Most serious students and researchers of "mind-power" phenomena will agree that what we are manifesting in the way of health, finances, and, in fact, every aspect of life at this very moment is the accumulative results of our *past* thinking. By that, I mean those thoughts that have been *lodged* in the subconscious. We've learned that these mental images we have been picturing all along are the basic reasons for our present negative or positive conditions.

An honest inventory of what we now have in our everyday life will give us a pretty good idea of what kind of thinking we have been engaged in and exactly what thoughts have penetrated into the executive factor of personality. If we like what we now possess then there's no need for a change in our thoughts. If not—well, that's what Concept Therapy is all about. As Dr. William Marth so aptly put it in his most unique talk during the 1961 Concept Therapy convention in Denver, "We get what we *image*, not necessarily what we deserve."

The purpose of this chapter is to offer for your consideration a couple of ideas concerning a technique for easier imaging. In other words, a method that may make it simpler for you to concentrate your thoughts. Concept Therapy teaches that if you can hold one image—to the exclusion of all other thoughts—for thirty-three and a third seconds, it will succeed in "sinking" into the subconscious and in due time it will manifest in your life. Dr. Fleet believes thirty-three and a third seconds of concentration is a long enough and significant period. It is my opinion that the mass of people in this old world of ours are "cursed" because they can only concentrate *consciously* on a single thought for just a few seconds at a crack. Their environment, family, friends, and, unfortunately, foes can on the other hand capture their attention for great lengths of time. I'll spell out the consequences of this situation and also report why I believe most of humanity finds it easier to focus their thoughts on the negative rather than the positive.

It was the week preceding Christmas in 1961 when my wife, daughter, and I were visiting Aum Sat Tat ranch, the international home of Concept Therapy. During this special holiday gathering in Texas, I had planned to query Dr. Fleet about a problem confronting me. My intention was not communicated to anyone, least of all the founder of Concept Therapy. Yet, when I met Dr. Fleet, quite by accident, he greeted me with these words: "Hello, Bill. I'm glad you could make it down for the holidays. I understand you have a question you'd like to ask me."

I let him finish his lunch at the Flamingo Grill, the ranch mess hall, before confronting him with my problem. "Frankly, Dr. Fleet, I'm having a heck of a hard time trying to concentrate my thought on one specific thing." This was my complaint. Despite what I considered to be diligent practice, I wasn't having much success controlling my concentration. "Maybe you can give me a couple of hints."

With a mischievous grin and a twinkle in his eyes, he asked me to *imagine* that I had twelve, little, crawling, wiggly "cooties" lined up on a table before me. I was to pick up these imaginary insects, one at a time, hold each one between my fingers and then *crush* the tiny bug into oblivion. Dr. Fleet instructed me to repeat the process until I had personally squashed the entire dozen make-believe "cooties" between my fingers.

I shivered involuntarily in disgust as I thought about the repulsive task before me. At that instant came the dawning. My thought had produced a *feeling*. It is a physiological fact (as well as psychological) that feeling tends to concentrate the mind. This information is of upmost importance in all mind-over-matter activity. Understanding the role feeling plays in fastening my thoughts, I could immediately see how to exclude superfluous ideas that flooded my mind whenever I attempted to consciously pinpoint my concentration on one specific goal and try to hold it for thirty-three and a third seconds.

The power of positive feeling has it all over plain, old positive thinking. I have often heard Dr. Charles K. Craig, California Concept Therapy instructor, say, "Feeling makes it the *present* perfect situation." I now know what he meant. By utilizing a thought-feeling combination, this writer has enjoyed a greater degree of image manifestation.

I titled this chapter *Image Drama* for a specific reason. Drama is a transliteration from a Greek word meaning action, or a thing done. Image Drama as I see it, can be defined, therefore, as a technique to activate a strong mental picture of something you want; a condition that needs changing or a desired character trait that needs changing into an equally strong corresponding feeling.

Again let me reiterate; the subconscious is triggered into action not by surface thoughts but by deep feelings. If you never in your life tasted a lemon, then when you just now read the word lemon, nothing happened. However, if you have tasted a lemon, chances are that your mouth started to salivate. If lemon doesn't do it, then how about a nice juicy dill pickle?

The citrus taste of a lemon is deeply rooted in your subconscious. When you thought about it, your glands reacted in a small degree for preparation of the real event. This is the degree of response that is needed in Image Drama. Perhaps you need a certain amount of money right now. Just thinking about it is not going to get the currency in your pocket. But *feeling* that you already have the money, *feeling* that the problem that was caused by not having the money has been solved—that could initiate a train of causation to bring you the desired cash.

After you have created a *detailed* mental picture of not only what you want but *how you would feel* after you actually received what you want, then it is necessary to take the first physical steps toward your objective. Remember this: *movement* must accompany thought and feeling.

How would it be most logical for you to receive extra money? Perhaps a raise in salary. How would you feel after a ten or twenty dollar a week raise? Besides that happy feeling, you would no doubt put a little extra something into the way you performed your daily task. Then start doing it now. Go about doing your work as if you already had the raise.

An acquaintance of ours, a housewife with three children, wanted to earn extra money selling her oil paintings. True, she had never before received a penny from any of her paintings but after taking Concept Therapy, she felt she could. First came the feeling that she had sold a painting for fifty dollars. Then came movement.

She noticed that a neighborhood restaurant exhibited various oil paintings on the walls. The restaurant management extended this courtesy to local professional artists. The name of the painter and the price wanted for the particular canvas accompanied the picture. This was a good place to start manifesting her image of getting money for her art work. She convinced the proprietor to hang her pictures on his wall.

Two weeks passed and still her paintings hung, attracting no customers. She kept up her feeling that they had been sold and the great feeling that she got from paying some long-standing bills with the cash the paintings had brought into the household. She also concentrated on the enjoyment her paintings were bringing the people who had purchased them.

Her concentrated thought-feelings did not waiver even after the restaurant owner removed her work from his walls and the paintings were back in her over-crowded apartment. Shortly afterwards a new neighbor happened to spot the canvases and made a cash offer. Before she realized what had happened she was selling paintings at a rate that astounded her "Doubting Thomas" husband.

You must have some kind of a plan of action that you believe will lead to the accomplishment of your image. Without this last step you have just an hallucination and not a workable image as Rev. Crump pointed out in one of his excellent articles in the *Beamer*, the monthly Concept Therapy publication.

It is my belief that anything that adds positiveness to our life should be used to its fullest. True pleasure enriches the

Soul and contributes to its growth. I don't think poverty propels one faster or farther along the path toward wisdom any more than I believe riches can buy greater awareness. It depends on your own basic concepts and what you do with what you have.

Albert Schweitzer, the great philosopher-missionary, believed that materialism and spirituality were not incompatible. "Behind materialism it is often possible to find great spiritual forces at work," he said some years before his death. It seems that we've inherited this guilt feeling that associates the possession of worldly comforts with the ways of the nonspiritual from the early days of Christianity.

In 1170, Petrus Waldus gave quite an impetus to the concept that being penniless was a prerequisite for a more perfect attunement with the Creator. After intensely studying part of the Bible, he rid himself of all his wealth and began life as an itinerant preacher of the Gospels. He and other early students of the Scriptures who foresook their riches to preach the Word set a certain standard that to this day has a far-reaching influence.

I most certainly do not believe that money is the root of all evil. However, making money your God is certainly a harmful practice. The person who successfully images perfect health, a good standard of living, and the ability to express himself as fully as possible is a much more valued member of our society than some ragged "holy man" who begs for his bread and bed.

We said that movement must accompany thought and feeling to manifest an image. It must be noted that there are two kinds of movement. There can be *real* movement, such as, looking in the want ads for a job, registering at employment agencies, and personally visiting as many places of employment as possible. Along with this kind of action you would hold the thought and feeling that you had a wonderful job paying you a fine salary.

Suppose, for some reason, that logical kind of movement

isn't possible; what to do then? In a most interesting taped lecture entitled, *Imagination*, Dr. Richard C. Schafer details another type. By the way, the Concept Therapy institute has an enormous library of taped lectures by instructors, as well as advanced students. These are made available at a nominal cost. I have found them most helpful and I treasure my collection.

It was the last chapter of Concept Therapy's psychiatry text that Dr. Schafer admitted hit him hard. Dealing with the three planes of energy, the instruction teaches that an image is also energy and goes on to suggest that with proper understanding of Concept Therapy principles, the highest of all healing methods—that of using pure ideas—can be utilized in affecting cures.

Most Concept Therapists have witnessed this kind of healing and it does at first strain the credulity until the realization of what is happening sinks in. The demonstrator of this type of healing calls the person who is in need of help up to the platform. Then he closes his eyes and "summons" from ETHERIA, or the world of ideas, the greatest surgeons, chiropractors, masseurs, medical doctors, teachers, philosophers, and clairvoyants to assist him.

Let me hasten to explain that when I used the word summon I meant the demonstrator *imagines* this distinguished grouping of entities are at his side ready to help. He asks the etheric clairvoyant to inform him of the trouble and what kind of assistance is needed. Then all of a sudden, an idea will come to him bringing the needed answers.

"For instance," Dr. Fleet writes, "by clairvoyance the healer demonstrating this technique will know that the patient has a condition that can be removed, say, by a surgeon. In this case, he pretends as though he is 'grabbing' the condition out. Then he throws it to one of the etheric surgeons with instructions to take care of it and bring about a cure. If he clairvoyantly determines that a patient is ill because of NOT KNOWING, he grasps the condition and throws it to one of the philosophers with instruction to take care of it, and the same with all the rest of them."

If this seems pretty "way out" to you, remember that modern science has just scratched the surface of the dynamics of which the mind is capable. The understanding that medical researchers have concerning how negative thoughts adversely affect the body is relatively new. The knowledge that thoughts can move inanimate objects is quite commonplace; that is, to students of mind-over-matter. Yet, straight-laced scientists condemn this as pure fantasy, just as they did the first reports of psychosomatic illness. Every time I hear an orthodox scientist pooh-pooh the borderline investigations, I am reminded that one eminent university professor, Simon Newcomb of Harvard, said, "Human flight is not only impossible, it is illogical." This was five years *after* the Wright brothers made their first historic flight.

Our friend, Dr. Schafer, was determined to prove or disprove to his satisfaction the contention that one could indeed manipulate idea-power to create health. This was before he gave up his successful chiropractic practice in New York State and moved his family to Aum Sat Tat ranch where he took over the printing of *The Beamer* and other graphic-art work for the institute. Never one to accept something just because someone said it was so, Dr. Schafer was a seeker of proof, and proof positive was what he discovered.

In his highly praised talk on imagination, he likened the technique needed to get past that barrier of limiting concepts (that negative "something" within the personality that separates most people from success) with the problem facing the captain of a lightweight football team attempting to score against heavier opposition. He can't crash through the center because he'd be crushed; so he must either pass or run around the end.

For one to get pass the "psychic wall" of guilt feelings, notions of inadequacies, and self-condemnation and enter into the realm of God-Power requires, says Dr. Schafer, *imagina-*

*tion.* "We think about the things foremost in our consciousness. In thought we can only choose that which is vibrating the most, so the average man is saddled with vibrations of fear, anxiety, and guilt. The negative emotions need very little stimulation from the outside to be brought up from the executive factor of the personality.

"How could I enter into this inner world and be able to command this great power to do my bidding? Thoughts fail one every time. Then the answer dawned on me from reading the last chapter in Concept Therapy's psychiatry text," says Dr. Schafer. The sentences that sparked the awakening for him were those that referred to the imaginative world of children. Dr. Fleet wrote: "Children automatically use the system of creating images and *living with them.* Jesus remarked that they were 'of the Kingdom of Heaven.'"

"When a child is at play, deeply engrossed in his world of make-believe, his thinking is only deductive from his imagination; not inductive," emphasizes Dr. Schafer, "but deductive!" Of course, he is right. My own little seven-and-a-half-year-old, Wendi Gayle, often pretends she is the Mommy of the household and acts out her chosen role accordingly. This type of play is not only healthy but it prepares her for the time when she will really be a mother. How do we prepare ourselves to master the world of ideas?

Dr. Schafer experienced a frightening situation that forever made him grateful for the ability to heal with ideas. His four-year-old daughter accidently swallowed an open safety pin. He immediately X-rayed her and to his horror saw that the pin was facing in the most dangerous possible position. For a minute he was helpless, immobilized, and then he remembered what he had learned about imaging. Immediately he swung into action.

He had his wife bring some bread and then fed it to his daughter. Then in his mind he imagined that the bread was completely engulfing the open safety pin. Further, he imagined that the pin was turning around and facing upwards so that when it passed through the bowels of his daughter it would do little harm.

Every four hours he X-rayed her and saw the safety pin slowly change direction and turn around. (I personally saw this amazing series of X-rays.) When the safety pin finally came out, his daughter was no worse for the experience. "This is an example," says Dr. Schafer, "of how one can use the imagination when 'scientific' means fail."

Dr. Fleet is an old hand when it comes to mind-over-matter. The following is just one out of hundreds of examples of his skill at directing the power within. Dr. O. W. Whittenberg, one of Concept Therapy's veteran instructors, was a first-hand witness and kindly relayed the following incident to me.

It was in 1949, when a Concept Therapist from Uvalde, Texas, who happened to be interested in South Texas winter gardening, was attending a Phase One class taught by Dr. Fleet. This student had about two or three hundred acres in garden vegetables and at the time was just about ready to begin the harvesting of fifty acres or so of fresh tomatoes. During one of the breaks in the middle of the class, he turned on the radio and heard the weatherman announce that the prediction was for freezing weather throughout South Texas.

He became concerned and told Dr. Fleet he thought he should go home at once to get additional help and pick as many of the vulnerable tomatoes as possible. Dr. Fleet understood the situation. Knowing that his student could salvage only a small percentage of the loss by going home, Dr. Fleet suggested remaining in the class. Here they would create an image through concentration, an image designed to prevent the temperature during the next few days from falling below 36°. The student agreed to stay and *the image was sent out*.

The next morning Dr. Fleet telephoned Dr. Whittenberg and asked for the temperature. Dr. Whittenberg knew nothing of the image experiment. He repeated the weather report he had just heard over the radio. A heavy frost had taken place over most of Southern Texas . . . *except* . . . in Uvalde County where the temperature had not gone lower than 36°. Local newspapers carried big write-ups on this odd weather phenomena that no one could understand.

When we were infants, the psychologists tell us, we possessed a God-like sense of power. It was only natural since our every desire was instantly satisfied. Whatever the time of day or night we wanted nourishment, we just opened our mouths and it wasn't many seconds before mother responded. Our soiled diapers became uncomfortable and all we did was cry out and an obliging parent came on the run.

We felt all-powerful. Everything we wanted to happen actually occurred. The world revolved around our actions. But as we became older and were bombarded with limiting, negative concepts, plus the usual share of frustrations, disappointments, and real or imaginary failures, we lost that feeling of being one with all life. You might say we "matured" into "logical thinking" adults enslaved to an association of ideas that more often than not kept us from a fuller, freer expression of life.

So let us now heed the Biblical advice to, "Be like a little child." With the power inherent in our imagination, we can again recapture that long-ago, lost feeling of being a mighty creator. We have the image-ability to create a Heaven right here and now. Too often this power has been used wrongly and instead of a Paradise we have manifested a living Hell. It is up to each of us to consciously choose what his imagination will create.

# CHAPTER SEVEN

# The Master Image

A CBS radio news broadcast reported the theory put forth by Dr. Aileen Lockhart of the Women's Physical Education Department of the University of Southern California. She contends that merely thinking about doing something makes the muscles act as though they were actually doing it, even though the person appears to be sitting perfectly still. "When one *sees* himself going through a sequence of action, such as hitting a golf ball, minute muscular action potentials in those muscles, which would be involved in actual movement, are invoked," Dr. Lockhart contends.

That would indeed seem to be the ideal way to improve your golf score. Just sit back in your easy chair, close your eyes, and start thinking. All it takes is a little time and concentration, the doctor says. If you're not a golfer, you can obtain more proficiency as a swimmer, tennis player, bowler, or boxer. However, Dr. Lockhart quickly points out that just thinking about it won't make an Arnold Palmer out of a duffer or a Sandy Koufax out of just anybody, since sports require endurance and strength as well as thinking; both physical and mental practice are necessary for improving performance.

Mental practice, she says, seems to aid in attaining smooth, easy, coordinated performance. Of course, the biggest drawback to all of this is simply the fact that most people can concentrate for only a few moments at a time on one specific thing. Dr. Lockhart emphasizes that one must think in terms of the *feel*.

In his best seller, *Psycho-Cybernetics*, Maxwell Maltz, M.D., refers to the aforementioned as "synthetic experiencing." He says we can learn to function successfully by experiencing success. "Memories of past successes act as 'built-in' stored information which gives us self-confidence for the present task," he writes.

How is it possible for us to synthesize experience? Maltz answers by saying, "The nervous system cannot tell the difference between an 'actual' experience and one imagined vividly and *in detail*." This seems pretty well to coincide with Dr. Lockhart's contention. If more proof is needed, I refer you to an interesting article printed a couple of years ago in a recognized scientific journal.

*Research Quarterly* reported an experiment done with three equated groups of basketball players. The first group practiced shooting baskets for twenty minutes a day. The second group did nothing with basketball for twenty days. The third group *thought* about shooting baskets for twenty minutes a day for the twenty days but did not actually handle the ball; they practiced, but only mentally.

By mental practice I mean that they closed their eyes and pictured themselves successfully shooting baskets. Which group do you think did best? At this point I'm sure you are ahead of me but be careful and don't let your mind trick you. The results are most interesting and point out something of enormous value.

Our first quintet, the cagers that got out on the hardwood and physically shot baskets improved 24 per cent. The boys who did nothing—the control group—made no improvement. The thing that set the researchers to wondering was the surprising results of the basketballers that utilized their imagination. The "mental-practicers" improved 23 per cent; just one point less than the squad that huffed and puffed, sweated and strained.

I now call your attention to a fascinating phenomenon called *ideomotor response*. Theologian William Carson Lantz, Ph.D. clarified this little understood mechanism of human makeup when he wrote about it some years ago in a medical magazine. "Sometimes, as a result of a dramatic dream, there is a muscle twitch, a catching of the breath, or a clenching of the eyes. Similar responses occur when one lets himself get involved in watching a drama or reading a fiction story, especially if he identifies himself with a particular character in the story. Involuntary twisting and turning sometimes result as one watches the football halfback twist and turn in broken field running. The passenger in a car sometimes moves his muscles as though he were driving. These are called ideomotor responses—spontaneous behavior based upon an idea implanted deeply in the brain."

Dr. Lantz points out that ideo-response can be seen in the common phenomenon of thinking so hard about waking up at a certain time the next morning that one actually does wake up at that time even without setting the alarm clock. This is motivation based on a vivid mental picture and what is so interesting, and to me downright exciting, is that it is able to *overcome* deep-seated habit patterns.

To further illustrate the ideo-response principle, Dr. Lantz suggests consideration of a man who has a well-ingrained habit of brushing his teeth after every meal. Suppose that on one particular evening this man is concentrating deeply on a portfolio of business papers as he eats. His mind is filled with economic matters, yet after he finishes his dinner he may very possibly move toward the bathroom sink spontaneously, automatically, naturally, or you might even say, subconsciously. If for a moment or so he happens to cease dealing mentally with his rational problems, he will no doubt become aware of the fact that he is making the movement toward the toothbrush rack.

What if he does not stop thinking about business matters? Then the awareness may never come at all and if so, he will later wonder whether he has brushed his teeth at all. I have a confession to make. This has happened to me and I had to go over the toothbrush to see if it was wet or not. A similar experience occurred while driving. One day I found myself at the corner of Sunset and Vine in Hollywood and for the life of me, I could not remember crossing the intersections at La Cienega, La Brea or Highland.

I wondered if I had stopped for red lights. Had I obeyed the traffic laws? Did I drive on the right side of the street? Apparently my subconscious had taken over and left my originative factor or deliberate mind, the reasoning part of me, to think about the coming day's activities, while it saw to it that my hands steered perfectly and all else went well.

We lived in Brentwood, a West Los Angeles suburb, for over five years. Each weekday I drove eastward on winding, multiple-curved Sunset Boulevard to my office at KNX-CBS radio in Hollywood. It wasn't often that I varied my route and morning and evening motoring became an ingrained habit pattern. It was in fact, a comfortable rut that allowed me to negotiate the required traveling to and from work with the least amount of mental effort thus giving me freedom to think about the day ahead.

After a while, I discovered to my increasing annoyance, that I would often forget to stop at a cleaning establishment once a week or so on my way to work. Even when I sometimes placed the bundle of clothes right next to me, I would often sail on right past the store only to glance at the neatly tied bundle when I was five miles beyond and it was too inconvenient to turn back. How could I remember to break the routine? Tie a string around my finger? Place the bundle on my lap? Those two alternatives seemed to me that I was admitting defeat. Dr. Lantz had a better idea; a method that would also be a valuable mental exercise.

By taking just half a dozen seconds before leaving in the

morning to see vividly a mental picture of myself stopping in front of the cleaning establishment, getting out, and depositing my clothes, I was able to overcome all conditioning to go on past, even though as I drove, my attention was focused intensely on some other stimulus. As potent a force as is repetition, it isn't always necessary in sinking a suggestion into the subconscious. Imagination, properly used, can be a shortcut to greater control of your subconscious powerhouse potential.

By vividly picturing (and that means imagining or thinking in terms of sensing and feeling images) we are implanting a seed of "future action" in the subcortical area. This not only initiates motor, sensory, or glandular response, but it can, Concept Therapy teaches, create a vibration that will attract into your life the picture you have so carefully cultivated. Admittedly, this is where orthodox psychology and conceptology part company. Science has not yet arrived at a full understanding of the fact that thoughts can not only affect the body but can alter conditions outside the physique.

Since we do live in an ocean of vibration, I find it easy to understand how "like attracts like." Much has been written on the subject of how by using your mind properly you can draw to you much more of life's many blessings. If one were to distill the voluminous words on this principle down to their essence, the technique would simply be as follows: Picture an image or feeling of abundance. Act as though this feeling of well-being permeated every inch of your being. Then be sure to allow prosperity to enter your life from *any* source. Especially be alert not to block blessings that might come from the most unlikely of areas.

Once, many years ago, when I was in desperate need of a writing position, my wife, June, suggested that a good idea was for me to buy the Sunday paper and scan the want ads for a suitable opening. I immediately rejected this action, since I felt that nobody in need of a writer would advertise in such a prosaic way. "After all, I'm not looking for a job as a box boy in some supermarket," I remarked contemptuously.

Since my imagining was apparently doing little good, I finally bought a paper and turned to the employment opportunities section. My eyes widened and my mouth fell open in astonishment. There it was, a small two-line advertisement that said: RETAIL WRITER WANTED. Underneath was a telephone number.

Nine o'clock on Monday morning, I called. Even though I was a radio and TV writer and hadn't the slightest idea what a retail writer wrote, I felt it still was worthwhile calling. "I'm sorry, but the newspaper advertisement was wrong," the voice on the other end of the line said. "What we really meant to advertise for was someone experienced in writing radio and television copy." I got the job.

After the proper incubation time, your image will become a reality if you haven't replaced the feeling-picture of abundance with a stronger image of impatience. Here's how that works. By wondering why the money you need hasn't come in yet or the job you desired hasn't manifested already or the healing has not yet occurred and feeling that perhaps it won't really work after all, you have created a "counter image," one that will negate what you consciously desire.

Consider the feeling of faith in the act of doubting. Think about that. After all, when one doubts that good fortune will come his way, is he not, in fact, implying faith in the negative? I had a friend who was a real, no-bones-about-it, "worry wart." He was quite vocal in his belief that little good would ever come his way. "I sure wish I was able to do this image bit," he lamented, "but I just can't do that sort of thing."

"Oh, yes you can," I said. He didn't believe me for a minute. What I said next stopped him in his tracks. "In fact, old buddy, you're one heck of a terrific imager, whether you know it or not." Momentarily speechless, he finally blurted, "What the Hell do you mean by that, Wolff?"

I felt he really was interested and would listen, so I told him, "Anyone who is constantly fearful, always looking on the gloomy side, and forever expecting bad breaks is an

78

experienced imager." His eyes told me to continue. "Just look at the mess some people call their lives and you can see the evidence of their image-ability."

He was receptive to my thesis and I went on. "The Law of Polarity instructs that anything which is bad or causes harm or unhappiness is at the same time capable of being beneficial. Fearing, doubting, or worrying is the negative aspect of mind-imagery. So anybody who can get scared, I mean really frightened of what the future holds in store for them, can also conjure up a powerful enough image to manifest a bright and wonderful tomorrow."

I stopped my preaching, that's what it was beginning to sound like, and let him think about what I had said. To this day I don't know how much an impression the idea I put forth made on him. One thing though, he was less willing to voice his misfortunes as before. It was said he even smiled on occasion.

I like to think he changed some of his fear into faith; it was not, however, my problem, what he did or did not do. Part of the pledge the advanced Conceptology student takes comes to mind as I think about just how involved one should become. The words are as follows: "I tread upon the work I do. I mount upon my slain self." I leave you to your own interpretation of those two lines.

Let us come back again to the Laws. I do this because nowhere in the scientific writings that I pored over or in the enormous amounts of lay literature on the subject I dissected did I find anything approaching a description of the seven Universal Laws. Just in case I haven't properly indicated in the preceeding chapters, I reiterate: It is the Laws that enable you to create a positive image that is *logical*. Remember, when an image or concept is logical, it then is, all other things being equal, capable of lodging in the subconscious and then, brother, you're in business!

Success, as we have said in the first part of this chapter, builds more success. This may seem strange but *one must practice having success.* Success is positive energy and since like attracts like, the more feelings of success you have the more actual success or positiveness will come your way. It has just been discovered by a team of psychologists and sociologists working with juvenile delinquents that by heaping praise and positive recognition on these so-called incorrigibles, that they changed dramatically from troublemakers to constructive members of society.

This is an example of letting youngsters taste, many for the first time, success. In effect, the researchers infused these deprived kids with large "doses" of positive energy and the results changed a lot of old-fashioned ideas about the cause and cure of delinquency. Reward is a great, if not the greatest, motivation for learning and modern educators are more and more utilizing this knowledge in new methods of teaching. Maybe that old adage, "You can catch more flies with honey than you can with vinegar" has a deeper meaning than we ever imagined.

We strengthen our ability to image by first manifesting minor wishes and then working up the scale to bigger and better things. At this point, there is nothing wrong with having your wishes realized. Who can deny the desirability of changing a life of failure or plodding mediocrity into one of triumph and achievement? I am of the opinion that it is valuable to learn how we can make our wishes come true, not for selfish, mundane reasons, but so that we can finally create and manifest what I prefer to call the MASTER IMAGE.

It is so very important that you be made aware that there must come a time when, as a truly mature soul, you will find little need for constantly wanting this or that, either for yourself or someone else. No longer will you be so anxious to change the negative into the positive, for you will more clearly see that perhaps a greater purpose than heretofore you ever understood, is being served. As Concept Therapy instructor, Katherine Calhoun, puts it: "Your list of 'druthers'

(I *druther* do this or I *druther* do that) will diminish considerably."

Unlike most people, your happiness will not be dependent on a person, place, or thing. Incessant desires for material things (and that includes wealth, health, and knowledge), will be replaced by an even greater longing. Yes, instead of wanting a better job, more money, perfect health, an understanding mate, or knowledge of metaphysical mysteries, etc., you will yearn with all your heart and soul for the "wall" to crumble so that you can at last be ONE WITH ALL OF LIFE.

I believe that as this particular expression of life labeled Man, or more accurately pre-Man, stumbled up from the dark, dim pit of his evolutionary beginnings, he discarded (no doubt for a good, if not fully understood reason) his complete dependency on instinct, that cybernetic, message-bearing link from which vital survival information emanated. The animal world's very existence was assured through the genius of the computer-like operation of instinct.

Is it not instinct that dictates at a particular time of year that the salmon depart from the open sea and make their way to the confines of the rivers? Besides the primary purpose of reaching proper locations for the act of propagation, they are able also to get rid of the tormenting sea-lice that cling to them in the ocean. The fresh water of the rivers are death to these gnawing, parasitic insects.

Consider also the canine. He doesn't have to be taught at his mother's knee or painfully figure out for himself that when he is sick he should eat grass or lick his wounds; he just performs. Were you aware that the cow and even the calf pretend to be dead so that nearby crows will pick the vermin from about their eyes and ears? Poultrymen tell me that chicks, as soon as they break the shell, peck at gravel to aid digestion. As that popular song of a few years back went, "They're only doing what comes naturally."

No doubt that the facts of life are transmitted through the genes, but unlike man, the animal is incapable of disobeying these "messages." When winter comes the birds fly south. Can you imagine a segment of, say, the robin population questioning the validity of its deep inclination to quit the land before the mantle of white covers the ground?

On the other hand, we have Life's premier creation, man. The human being has conquered his environment. Instead of adapting to it as do the animals, he changes it to suit his peculiar wants and needs and now he is about to leave the mother planet and explore strange, far-away worlds. Who can deny the nobility of such a life expression? Yet, even though he knows beyond the shadow of a doubt that he should not overeat, he does so anyway. His conscience crys out for him to refrain from certain destructive acts but, poor creature, he pleads that he is helpless to stop. He gets a "hunch" and laughs it off. He blithely ignores inclinations from within until he is completely deaf to that "still, small voice."

Not a day passes that mankind, for the most part, isn't engaging in some kind of activity that leads to a premature demise. This then, is the price paid for not being at one with life, for not being in harmony with it, and for being unable to perceive and heed the constant stream of messages coming in—communication that could answer those critical questions and solve the most pressing of problems.

Well then, just how do we get *in tune with the Infinite?* Can it be done? I believe, or rather, I hope so. I'm trying, and that's for sure. Without being too immodest, I can truthfully report that some slight gains are visible and that encourages me to continue. However, one can't just become in tune by brute force. It's a step-by-step proposition. One would indeed be wise to heed the advice to *go slow.* Being impatient, even when it's to make perfect union with God, penalizes the soul. That would be a case of doing the wrong thing for the right reason.

As professed "seekers after Truth," let's try to understand first what we are after. There is a possibility that if we really *knew* what it was we were so anxious to attain to, it might

82

conceivably put a damper on our eagerness. Take, for instance, the fundamentalist minister of the Gospel; that fire-and-brimstone, Bible-thumping preacher-man who knows beyond a shadow of a doubt that his and only his particular denominational interpretation of Scriptures is *the* truth. Reason tells me that he isn't so much interested in getting in tune with the Infinite as he is to get everyone else in tune with his beliefs. And so it is with most every other religious leader and, I dare say, with many metaphysical truth teachers as well.

I like to take my cues from observable life and since the animal obeys his instinct, man, too, should let intuition be his guide. Of course, man has a lot of groundwork to lay before he is in any kind of position to trust his inner inclinations. My theology is as follows: God, or whatever you wish to label the First Cause, is the Supreme originative factor and it therefore follows that we should be as perfect an executive factor as possible. Being able to do so would assure one a life of perfect fulfillment, truly, a heaven on earth. However, I do not mean a life free from challenges, for that would be Hell.

Action is an integral part of imaging and so when you're in the act of mental creation, keep in mind that it is what you do that counts and not only what you think. Learn to respond to the inclinations that will start to flow from the *Source*. Try to give up, at least for a while, your inherited religious concepts or metaphysically taught idea of God. There is a chance that a few of your basic beliefs are to some extent incorrect. Don't block fresh information that might be on the threshold of your consciousness. It was the great philosopher Descartes who said, "If you would be a real seeker after truth, it is necessary that at least once in your life you doubt, as far as possible, all things."

Kneeling in prayer is the symbolic act of the Soul relinquishing for a few seconds the originative role and obeying the admonition to "be still." If you're constantly talking on the telephone, nobody can get through to you, despite the importance of their message. They'll be getting a busy signal every time they try to call and no doubt eventually will forget about ever trying to reach you. Get the analogy? The whole purpose and intent is dissolved when the mind is as cluttered with trivia when you're on your knees as when you're driving, shopping, or gulping down your food.

A continuous stream of thoughts spring up in your mind because you have been "programmed" to react to *outside* conditions. Perhaps we do have more distractions now, but people down through the ages have had to overcome this same kind of conditioning. This is why much emphasis has been placed on meditation. Although meditation is a preparation for inner communication, I don't believe it's the end-all, the magic panacea, as some claim. But it is vital that we do learn to cease thinking (originating) for periods of time and train ourselves to halt reacting to exterior stimuli. Doing this opens the channels for intuition to bridge the chasm separating the finite from the Infinite. To this end we employ the MASTER IMAGE.

# CHAPTER EIGHT

# Conversation with a Cosmic Man

It was in 1931 when Thurman Fleet of San Antonio, Texas, a retired army captain with a distinguished World War I record and also a successful chiropractor boasting a growing practice, experienced what is generally regarded as an "Illumination." For seven days and nights he seemed to have been placed in a consciousness superior to his ordinary state. It has been said that during this period of time, the entire panorama of life was revealed to him as an image, and he felt "instructions" to return to his normal consciousness and gather up the truth connected with this image. He was instructed further, to put this truth together and return with it to the "higher plane of consciousness."

I don't know for a fact who it was that instructed him or where the higher plane of consciousness is located. There were those who accused Dr. Fleet of temporary insanity. I have my own personal theory and, as a matter of fact, so do many well-known, scientifically accredited authorities. Some of our leading "mind investigators" take the kind of mystical, visionary, or cosmic experience Fleet had quite seriously. I know that I do.

Sidney Cohen, M.D., in his extremely interesting book, *The Beyond Within*, explores this type of transcendent experience with much scientific interest. He points out that Dr.

Maslow, another respected psychological researcher, has reported that it is the healthiest individual who encounters peak moments most frequently. He even goes so far as to say that in our emotional evolution the missing link between the anthropoid ape and *Mature Man* might be present-day man.

Last year at CBS Radio in Hollywood, I had the opportunity to personally ask Dr. Cohen if he believed that a person might have a *true* "cosmic consciousness" experience. He said, "How else do you suppose our great religions came into being?"

Following his week of "cosmic consciousness," Dr. Fleet explained that he had been "given" specific instructions to go back down the Path to the lower plane and find the *truth*, wherever it may be, and put it together as a completed whole and then bring it back to the higher plane. To this task he has devoted his life. Now, thirty-four years later, he has become famous to thousands of truth seekers throughout the world as the founder of Concept Therapy, a philosophy of life claimed to contain the wisdom of the ages correlated into a compact, easily understood course of instruction. Concept Therapy dramatically changed my life for the better, and ever since my first encounter with this remarkable philosophy, I have been intrigued by the story of the man responsible for its creation.

My first personal contact with Dr. Thurman Fleet was in Chicago, less than a year after my initial exposure to Concept Therapy. This was in 1955 and by then a half-dozen or so teaching teams were scheduling classes throughout the United States and Canada. The emphasis was on the work rather than the person responsible for correlating the principles being taught. I imagine that my wife and I were no different from many others, who for no apparent reason assumed that Concept Therapy's founder was long laid to rest.

It came as a mild surprise and large delight to learn that *the man* was not only much alive, but would be visiting Chicago. He was touring the country giving psychiatric therapy instruction (Concept Therapy's special brand, not to be confused with the orthodox type) to professionals engaged in the healing arts. My wife and I, a little reluctantly, since we had no healing aspirations, enrolled in the three-day course mainly to get a close-up, in-person view of Dr. Fleet. It turned out to be quite an interesting experience. Since then, I have had the opportunity of hearing him teach many times and also to meet him on a more personal and intimate basis.

Dr. Fleet's contribution to the world of ideas, I believe, is a rich and intriguing one, well deserving of continued and close examination. The interview or dialogue presented here is for the most part based on several recent meetings I had with him. One was during a trip he made to California to visit his daughter and son-in-law; another was in between sessions of Concept Therapy's twenty-first International convention held in St. Louis.

WOLFF: In your own words, Dr. Fleet, what is it exactly that you teach?

FLEET: Our teachings are listed under the names of Concept Therapy and Conceptology. The word concept, in the last analysis, means ideas, and therapy means working with. We teach our students how to work more effectively with ideas. One who understands the principle behind our teachings, finds he can heal with ideas.

WOLFF: Heal what?

FLEET: Bodies, minds, and souls. By healing I mean not only restoring good health to a diseased body or bringing balance to an emotionally confused mind, but also to change a life that is filled with frustration and lack into one that enjoys the abundance of a positive, rewarding existence.

WOLFF: I understand that a great many doctors as well as laymen subscribe to your philosophy. In fact, this work was originally intended for professionals engaged in healing and then later others were allowed to take the instruction. But isn't it true that many doctors in the past have differed with your approach to healing?

FLEET: Yes, that was the case in the past, but now in many of the healing sciences there is an increasing awareness and recognition of the factors of psychosomatic illness. This reveals the influence of a nonphysical element in the functioning process of the body. Various names are given to this element. Some call it the "Mind" without explaining what the mind is. Others call this element the Soul and nowhere can one get a factual idea of what constitutes a Soul. Mental students say the element is the subconscious mind, but again there is no one to explain the real meaning of this term.

WOLFF: Isn't it true that psychiatrists and psychologists seem to be working with this element with varying degrees of success?

FLEET: Yes, we are cognizant that many healers approach the problem of alleviating disease by discussion rather than treatment with drugs. Then there is suggestion which plays its part in combatting this nonphysical element as evidenced by hypnosis and those practitioners who heal knowingly or unknowingly by employing suggestive therapy. Concept Therapy endeavors to give its students a logical understanding of this element which can disturb the harmonious functioning of the human body so that the element which can cause disease may be rendered harmless by the person who understands it.

WOLFF: From what I gather so far in our discussion, you are advancing the case for greater emphasis on the nonphysical part of man.

FLEET: It is the psychic nature of man which should be understood more than the physical, for the latter is so very much dependent upon the former. Modern psychology has thrown much light on the psychic nature of man. Concept Therapy is therefore the study of a mysterious element in the psychic nature that has to this date baffled understanding.

WOLFF: What started you investigating this so-called unknown element?

FLEET: Well, that goes back to when I was classified totally disabled by the army because of my World War I wounds received in France. I was an infantry captain. Long about 1929, the medical men had just about given me up. They told my wife that I had a three-inch vortex pressure on the brain from shrapnel I received in the trenches, and it might kill me at any time.

WOLFF: How did this affect your life?

FLEET: Believing I was completely incapacitated, we moved to a home in Corpus Christi, Texas. I spent most of my days in an old rocking chair on the front porch waiting to die. I didn't want to die, but the M.D.'s said they could do nothing for me. One day I remembered I had seen a chiropractor's sign downtown. I decided I had nothing to lose by giving that a try.

WOLFF: You started chiropractic treatments?

FLEET: Yes, and I began to improve. I was so pleased with the results that I enrolled in the Texas Chiropractic College myself. I graduated and began a new career. In my years of practice, I noticed that some of my patients could not get well regardless of the treatment they received.

WOLFF: What did you make of that observation?

FLEET: I suspected at the time that it was some unknown cause responsible for their trouble. My training and own research along those lines led me to suspect an unknown element operating in people that caused the majority of their diseased conditions.

WOLFF: What happened then?

FLEET: I wanted answers and so I began to study. I studied so intently on this that I purchased whole libraries from the army. I would classify each book as being either about the body, the mind, or the soul, which I would keep. After separating these thousands of books in their component files, I began to go through them, extracting the part that might lead me to a greater understanding of this unknown element. Every available minute was devoted to the search. Day and night I would go through these books. Perhaps I studied too hard because I had a most unusual experience.

WOLFF: What was this experience?

FLEET: I seemed to have had an "Illumination" in which this element was revealed to me in all of its clarity. This experience, call it what you may, lasted seven days and seven nights, at the end of which I was back in my normal consciousness. I knew beyond a shadow of a doubt that I had made a great discovery. However, I was unable at the time to explain it or put it to work.

We'll return to our conversation after more closely examining the strange experience that so altered Dr. Fleet's life. Luckily, we have an eyewitness in the person of Dr. Calvin P. Wright, Dr. Fleet's brother-in-law. On a recent teaching trip to Los Angeles, he kindly permitted me to question him at great length and he was most generous with detailed information concerning Dr. Fleet's illumination.

Dr. Wright, the head of psychiatry for the Concept Therapy Institute, is a remarkable and colorful figure in his own right. His classes are always jam-packed and highly praised. I've gained a great deal of psychological help from his instruction, as well as his personal counseling. He told me that he was fifteen years old when he first met Dr. Fleet, who was then courting Delia Wright, Cal's older sister.

A friendship that has meant the world to Dr. Wright began then, and he readily admits that in those early days he literally worshiped this dynamic young man who seemed to possess such unique abilities. As a high school student in Douglas, Arizona, Wright was given an assignment by his teacher that had him stumped. He had to write an essay on friendship. He told Fleet of his homework and asked for some help. For a moment, Fleet was silent, then with few pauses, he rattled off an essay on the subject so fast, that young Cal Wright could hardly write it down.

"Friendship is a mutual agreement between all classes of

90

humanity. Sometimes it flowers into love . . ." That was all of the essay Wright can recall. "My teacher was so thrilled with the paper, she had me read it to the class and then go into some of the other rooms to read it," Wright remembers. "Finally, I confessed that it wasn't my work, but that of my sister's boyfriend."

George Thurman Fleet (he later dropped his first name) was absolutely the last person in the world you would expect to be a spiritual trailblazer. He was a man's man and subject to the normal pleasures of healthy young males. He gravitated toward a military career and fit in well as a professional soldier. However, even at an early age he developed a natural talent for organization. He also had a keen memory, inexhaustible energy, and was reputed to be quite intuitive.

An insight into the man can best be had by viewing Fleet, the youth. In 1915, as a corporal in the U.S. army stationed on the Arizona-Mexican border, a small incident occurred that shed some small light on Fleet's character. He and an officer were patrolling a section of the barren, sun-baked terrain when in the distance Fleet spotted a man crawling along the Mexican side.

"Lieutenant!" Fleet called out, "Looks like somebody's in trouble or something." He guided his mount closer to the figure who now saw the two horsemen. Desperately the ragged, bandoleered Mexican begged for water. The Americans were still too far away to actually hear anything, but it didn't take much imagination to know what the man wanted.

Fleet spurred his horse forward. "Corporal, you reign up, do you hear me? Stay away from that Mexican," the officer commanded.

The young soldier obeyed looking questioningly toward the Lieutenant. "Our orders are not to cross the border. We're to keep away from Mexican nationals. These people are fighting each other and that's obviously a rebel who got lost from his troop," the older man reasoned.

"Sir," Fleet said, looking straight into the Lieutenant's eyes,

91

"What happens if I ride over and give him my canteen?" The officer, momentarily startled by the question, recovered quickly enough to sputter, "Mister, you do that and you'll be fined $120.00 and it'll go on your record that you disobeyed Battalion orders."

Fleet, stony-faced and silent, moved toward the Mexican, a twelve-year-old boy. He dismounted and gave the lad his canteen. Then he returned to the officer's side. Fleet never questioned the justice of his punishment. As a soldier, he knew what to expect when disobeying an order, but it did not dissuade him from doing what he knew he had to do.

Let's pick up Thurman Fleet's story long after he had laid aside his uniform. We look into his life on a day like no other day he had ever experienced. Actually, this day would merge into six other days that would leave their indelible mark on the man and his world. We view the events of that period through the eyes of a witness.

The morning of December 17th started much the same as any other day for Cal Wright. In the kitchen of his apartment, he was leisurely sipping a second cup of coffee and thinking about the coming holiday. He still had to finish up his Christmas shopping and he was wondering about going downtown. San Antonio, like other cities in Texas and throughout the nation in 1931, faced serious economic problems, but still most of the shops and stores this time of the year were crowded.

Cal's musing was abruptly interrupted by five-year-old George Fleet. The boy burst into the room and cried out, "Brother, Brother (Cal's nickname), come quick! Mommy says Daddy is sick." Then the youngster turned around and dashed back out, high-tailing it down the street for home. Behind him, breathing hard, came Cal Wright. Chilly as it was that winter day, he hadn't stopped to slip on a sweater; he was unaware of the frigid weather. All that ran through his mind was the frightening prospect that Thurman might be ill.

The Fleet residence, a rambling, four-bedroom brick house surrounded by large hackberry trees, was just a block away. The fifty-foot porch that ran the length of the house provided shelter for the many boxes upon boxes of books that Fleet had been reading. During the last year, he had spent as much as twenty hours a day poring over volume after volume.

Wright bounded up the stairs of the porch and without stopping to knock entered the large living room. Describing the scene, he said, "The first thing that made me aware that something had happened was when I saw Fleet. He had shaved off his moustache." This may seem rather insignificant on the surface, but Cal was well aware that his brother-in-law was more than just a little bit vain when it came to his pencil-thin moustache. Cal also noticed that Thurman was pale and there was this intent, glittering sparkle in his eyes; however, he did speak rationally and this relieved Cal somewhat, that is, until Thurman started making certain statements.

"Cal, I've tuned in on the secret of all healing," Fleet quietly informed him. Startled as he was, Wright recalls, "Thurman didn't seem to be ecstatic about this strange turn of events. He was extremely serious and this one statement seemed to absorb his whole personality."

Fleet, pacing up and down, finally turned and left the living room and entered the den, with Cal trailing behind him. He began to worry in earnest about Fleet's condition as he observed him talking with "invisible entities" of some kind. From what he observed, Fleet reacted in a way that indicated the "entities" seemed to be answering him back.

Cal Wright thought it would be best that Fleet not be left alone and spent most of the seven days by his side, bedding down on the living room sofa. Along about the sixth day, at dawn, Fleet awakened Wright, saying, "Cal, do you hear that music?" Wright sat up, rubbed his eyes and strained to hear. After a few minutes he sadly admitted, "Thurman, I can't hear anything, except maybe the crickets outside."

Fleet made Cal stand up and then, linking arms with him, the two walked around the living room side by side, seemingly in tune to the "Music." This was the first "Slump," a form of musical therapy practiced by "Beamers" or Concept Therapy followers. The word SLUMP stands for: Souls Live Upon Many Planes. It is a vital element in the philosophy's mystique and an invaluable method of impregnating the Master Image indelibly on the consciousness. I better add that the music now employed can be heard by all. However, it's music that one would never think of using for such a purpose.

Mrs. Fleet had tried unsuccessfully to get Thurman to eat during that seven-day period. He even refused grapefruit, his favorite food. Occasionally, he would sip some water. Dr. Wright observed that physically, Fleet had undergone a metamorphosis. "He seemed . . . how can I put it . . . *etheric*. It was as if you could see right through him or like you could put your finger right through his body. That's how much he changed."

The illumination lasted from the 17th of December through the 24th. Wright, well-acquainted with psychological theories of the day, feared at first that Fleet had developed a religious complex. As time passed, however, he began to understand a little of the magnitude of this enigmatic happening. Certain prophecies, predictions of things to come, made by Fleet in his altered state of consciousness began to take place. Predictions, such as: The closing of the nation's banks, the formation of the CCC camps, social security legislation, the creation of the gold depository at Fort Knox., etc.

Following the paranormal episode, Fleet was a man possessed with the desire to more fully understand the true nature of his strange step into *Cosmic Consciousness*. To this day, some thirty-five years later, he is still perfecting his comprehension. It is because of this that Concept Therapy remains fresh and alive, in step with the world and free from the stagnating effect of unalterable dogma.

Fleet's reputation as a healer spread. Even though he

opened his office doors only in the evening between seven and nine, as many as 120 patients crowded his clinic during those two working hours. "It was the power of suggestion through the spoken word that healed," says C. P. Wright. "Some of San Antonio's most important and influential citizens were his patients, including several ladies whose husbands were leading medical doctors in the community."

Dr. Fleet tried desperately to give his knowledge to the established healing professions. As can be expected, the medicos scoffed at him and refused to listen. Even chiropractors denied him a hearing. He approached James Drain, president of the Texas Chiropractic College, one of the few people who had observed Fleet during his week of illumination. "Dr. Drain, I want to teach your students how they can really heal people no matter what part of the body they adjust."

The school head was sympathetic to Fleet. Personally, he liked the thirty-six-year-old retired army captain, who had for a short time been a student of his. But he had fought too hard to bring a measure of respectability to his profession to be swept off his feet and allow some mysterious "Mumbo-Jumbo" taught in his classrooms. Dr. Fleet persisted and finally the older man said, "I'll tell you what, Fleet. Take it or leave it, but this is the deal. Work with this for ten years, then come back with the results. If you can prove that what you have really works, I'll help you all I can to promote it."

Ten years, almost to the day, Fleet drove up to the college in an old pick-up truck, borrowed for the occasion. He and a helper then proceeded to unload cardboard boxes, filled to capacity with hundreds of black-framed letters of endorsements from people who had testified they had greatly benefited from Fleet's methods. The boxes were plunked down unceremoniously in front of a startled Jim Drain. Smiling, Fleet said, "Well, Doc, you wanted proof, you said. Here it is."

Recovering his composure, Drain picked up a few of the framed letters at random and studied them. A smile slowly spread across his face, then, looking up, he said, "I know what you've been doing. We've all been watching you and now I'm going to keep that promise I made to help put this thing . . . this secret of yours, before my profession." Fleet, overjoyed, grabbed Drain's hand and shook it vigorously.

A class was organized to be held during the Texas Chiropractic College homecoming in 1944. About fifty doctors sat in on the instruction given in the old south terrace room of the Gunter Hotel in San Antonio. That was the beginning. Those first students were so impressed with what they heard that they decided to band together and do their utmost to perpetuate this teaching. Thousands upon thousands have followed in the footsteps of those original fifty. Throughout the United States and Canada came the seekers, the sincere, and the merely curious. Those who stayed have built a mighty international organization dedicated to the Truth, *that Truth that makes men Free.*

# CHAPTER NINE

## Conversation Continued

WOLFF: During your illumination, Dr. Fleet, you said that certain things were revealed to you. Exactly what was revealed?

FLEET: "Psychically" I received a highly condensed version of what we are now putting into eight separate texts.

WOLFF: I heard the story that you wrote down what you received in a strange and, to you, a completely unfamiliar language. Is this true?

FLEET: Yes, it is. I started writing on every scrap of paper I could get . . . even the wallpaper. Later, someone suggested we send the strange scribblings to a professor of ancient language. We did this and it was then that we discovered I had written it in Sanskrit.

WOLFF: What happened after the week of illumination?

FLEET: Then came years of effort trying to understand what had been placed in my consciousness; the reading by the thousands of books pertaining to health. Finally, the whole picture cleared up in my conscious mind and I was then able to write textbooks on this element, which I did, and utilized with great success in my chiropractic practice.

WOLFF: I imagine your practice grew.

FLEET: It became so large that I was almost unable to handle it. I had promised that if what I had discovered really worked,

I would organize classes and teach it so that all could benefit.

WOLFF: Did you plan on charging for this instruction?

FLEET: I tried giving this knowledge away free but soon learned an amazing thing about people. Little value is placed on something that costs them nothing. It was in 1937 when I started traveling around the country teaching Concept Therapy to doctors, mostly chiropractors.

WOLFF: Were the classes largely attended?

FLEET: Anywhere from three students to fifty at a time. Following the class the students would form study groups which we called "On-The-Beam" clubs. The club members identified themselves as "Beamers." These clubs were then incorporated into a national organization (later international). At this time we have over 250 of these clubs chartered. Once a year, we have an international "On-The-Beam" convention held in some centrally located city.

WOLFF: There's a story . . . perhaps a better word would be legend . . . making the rounds concerning your method of gleaning pertinent data from the thousands of books you studied to get at the needed information comprising the Concept Therapy text. Did you have to read every word on every page of every book?

FLEET: I would glance at a page and it seemed like my attention would be riveted on one particular paragraph or just a few words that would fit in with the picture that I was establishing. It seemed as if it was automatic that I would instantly recognize what I would need out of the book, much like you would recognize a friend in a crowd.

WOLFF: Tell me something more about the text material. What is its objective?

FLEET: To teach a sincere seeker how to better his or her life, to give the student a greater understanding of his personality. It begins by showing how the nonphysical element exists in the electron, the atom, the molecule . . . the substance. We show how it created the minerals, the vegetable and animal worlds, and finally the human world. The teaching

98

follows the methods of science. Having established that this nonphysical element is within each person, we then begin to explain the component parts of the human personality and show their action, one upon the other. The instruction outlines the laws under which this nonphysical element works while in the body and teaches the student how he or she can work with and not against this element.

WOLFF: Suppose that because of ignorance you work against this element, what happens?

FLEET: Just look around at the misery prevailing in many, too many lives. People working against this element attract frustration, phobias, disease, poverty, and even untimely death. I would say that almost everyone who does not have proper instruction on how to work with his nonphysical element is working against it.

WOLFF: What subject matter is covered in the other texts?

FLEET: In "Phase One" we break the human personality down to its component parts and explain the working of each to show how ideas, thoughts, and things affect the person. This is great knowledge, especially for those engaged in healing.

WOLFF: How so?

FLEET: The doctor will find how psychosomatic conditions originate and how they may be eliminated.

WOLFF: Do you teach hypnosis?

FLEET: We thoroughly instruct our students in hypnosis so that they can become aware of how an idea detrimental in nature, can be transmitted from one to another, and exert its destructive force within the body. The student is given a method by which he can insulate himself, so to speak, from persons or from his environment. Our students become familiar with all details of how to penetrate, contact, and direct the power which lies within each person's subconscious depths.

WOLFF: What is the goal . . . the end results hoped for by a person seriously engaged in the study of Concept Therapy?

FLEET: I hope it is the sincere desire to attain to the Fourth Dimensional consciousness, that awareness which some men call Cosmic Consciousness.

WOLFF: Then your work in its entirety is designed specifically to bring about that awareness in your students. You described a couple of your volumes. What are the others that help instruct the individual eager for a taste of the cosmic?

FLEET: In "Phase Two" psychoanalysis and psychiatric principles are employed to inform a student of the detrimental, hidden factors lurking in the subconscious which he inherited or acquired and which hinder him from having a happy, healthy life. Once this knowledge is gained, a person is able to look within and detect these traits and begin a process of elimination, a housecleaning you might say, which when completed will do away with self-caused disease.

WOLFF: Alright, so much for "Phase Two." Now suppose the student likes what he has learned so far and continues his instruction. What is given to him in "Phase Three?"

FLEET: This gives a description of the inner battle that all human beings fight. Sigmund Freud also taught of this battle, between the inner and outer consciousness. This phase of our work is a lifesaver for anyone whose subconscious is constantly upsetting the applecart. It's also here where we teach in detail about the seven Universal Laws of Life.

WOLFF: You say, battle. What battle are you talking about and who are the participants of this struggle?

FLEET: The battle within of which I speak is the one raging between the carnal and the spiritual nature. It's the source of much unhappiness and misery . . . mental, physical, and spiritual. Once the full picture of this battle is gained, the person is able, at long last, to look forward to a release from habits which tend to drag him downward. He'll know that a character change is necessary and he will have the required knowledge to make this change.

WOLFF: What's next in the scale?

FLEET: "Phase Four." This initiates the student into a higher

100

consciousness which is called the cosmic or the consciousness of the one life. Here we give the rules that the student must inculcate into his or her life in order to serve what you might call a probationary period of trying to go through the gate into the higher life.

WOLFF: What do you mean probation?

FLEET: It's an old metaphysical term describing certain steps a student takes on the "Path of Attainment."

WOLFF: Attainment to what?

FLEET: To a higher consciousness. The student is placed on probation for a while and then, if he is found worthy, with self-discipline and understanding, he then goes to the next test which is taught in "Phase Five."

WOLFF: What is this test?

FLEET: The "enlightenment" process, and it explains the mystery of the teachings of the great Masters who gave us all our religions.

WOLFF: What exactly does the Concept Therapy student become enlightened about?

FLEET: He becomes enlightened as to the real meaning of the word *life*. He actually becomes conscious of what all the great Masters of thought experienced when their consciousness took a jump from the third into the fourth dimension. He eagerly awaits for the great event to happen in his own life ... and it will if he is truly sincere and applies himself.

WOLFF: What happens to the student when he attains to the fourth dimension of awareness?

FLEET: Why, he becomes a "master of matter," and works with it much as a potter works with clay. An entirely new life unfolds, a higher life, as he becomes able to blend his consciousness into the "one life" and render himself obedient to its laws.

WOLFF: So far, you've touched on Concept Therapy, Phases One, Two, Three, Four, and Five. What about Phase Six; what does it teach?

FLEET: This actually gives the medium by which the student can enter into this "One Life." We call it "initiation."

WOLFF: Initiation into what?

FLEET: The higher realm of consciousness.

WOLFF: Is this the last phase of your work?

FLEET: No. The final step is "Phase Seven." This completes the instruction.

WOLFF: I'm rather anxious to know what that part of your work is all about.

FLEET: That covers the illumination process. This is where the student's consciousness is filled with light. He has all the answers now. He can take his place in the "Higher Order."

WOLFF: I don't quite understand; what higher order are you talking about?

FLEET: These people have been known throughout the ages as the "illuminata" and they have given the world its great truths.

WOLFF: What in relation to existing religious teachings do you consider the higher consciousness you've been talking about to be?

FLEET: I have studied the six major religions deeply to get at the answer to that particular question, Bill. I'm convinced now that the men who brought the religions to us—Jesus, Moses, Buddha, etc.—were more or less men like you and me who for some unknown reason went into this higher consciousness. When they came out of the cosmic area to their normal human consciousness, they tried to tell others what they experienced there. And from that came all of our great religions.

WOLFF: Please define what you mean by the higher consciousness. What do you think it is?

FLEET: I personally believe it is another dimension of consciousness that awaits the human being who wants to study along that line, much like the higher understanding of mathematics that awaits the student who will take the necessary training to go into the upper echelons of mathematics.

102

WOLFF: Can this higher consciousness be actually attained through study?

FLEET: Yes, I firmly believe that the sincere student who will study these eight Concept Therapy and Conceptology texts and puts those principles to work in his or her daily life, will over a period of time enter into the fourth-dimensional consciousness, which to me is what has been taught as the Kingdom of God.

WOLFF: What are your ideas concerning God?

FLEET: I believe that the word God and the word Soul mean one and the same thing. To make that clearer let's take something we are all aware of, for instance, ice. Say we have a block of ice. Everyone knows you can take a block of ice and by applying energy (heat) you can change it into water. I believe the same applies to the human Soul and what men call God. They differ only in degree. The Bible states we're all Gods in the making. With such knowledge as we teach in Concept Therapy, the person who will apply it rigidly in his life will then become more Godlike each day. While he will never become what most individuals concede as God, he will change in consciousness so that he will express a more Godlike life. That is the purpose of all the religions of the world; to bring you into a close harmony with the "One Life," which men call God.

WOLFF: How do you explain why you went into the higher consciousness without preparation?

FLEET: I honestly don't know why I was "yanked" into it.

WOLFF: What do you mean "yanked" into it?

FLEET: I would describe it as a step of discontinuity that I had and am unable to explain. But while I was in that fourth dimension it seemed that the secrets of the universe, insofar as man's health and happiness is concerned, were revealed to me.

WOLFF: What were your exact feelings, physically and emotionally, I mean? I realize it was over thirty years ago when you had this experience, but can you recall how you felt?

FLEET: I can remember being engulfed in a terrific bright light, and it seemed as if all life were one. Every answer was there . . . available.

WOLFF: What kind of answers?

FLEET: Those that men and women seek throughout their life. It was all there and it was indelibly impressed on my subconscious tissues. Then when I came back to my normal consciousness, I could not remember it, except in part. I had this dynamic desire to find out just what happened to me. It took years of research and study to get it from my subconscious up to my conscious. I now feel that I know, although there are many questions that my students ask that, to be perfectly truthful, I must admit that I do not know the answers to.

WOLFF: What is the one question people most ask you?

FLEET: Is there life after death?

WOLFF: Dr. Fleet, do we survive bodily death?

FLEET: I do not know.

# CHAPTER TEN

*They Came to Learn
and Stayed to Teach*

From all walks of life and from every religious persuasion, as well as from the ranks of the "nonbelievers," the students came, searching for answers, seeking cures, and hoping to clear away the confusion that clouded their lives. Some were so helped by this unique philosophy that they felt duty-bound to spread the teaching. In many cases, these men and women gave up the materialistic security of lucrative careers to bring Concept Therapy to Chicago and Montreal; to Deadwood, South Dakota and Grand Rapids, Michigan; to Los Angeles, California and Grants Pass, Oregon; to Milwaukee, Wisconsin and Savannah, Georgia.

One such person who abandoned the safety and security of conventionality was E. L. Crump. He graduated from the University of Tennessee with a Bachelor of Science in Electrical Engineering. Having been in the top of his class, he was accorded the opportunity as one of two honor students to work for the General Electric Company at Schenectady, New York. While in their research department, he enjoyed the privilege of serving under the leadership of the great scientific genius, Charles P. Steinmetz. Crump told me, "During the whole ten years of my activity as an electrical engineer, while working with the great *physical power* of electricity, I was also tremendously interested in the *power* that directed man's mind."

Giving up his scientific work, he went to the Candler School of Theology, Emory University, Atlanta, Georgia. While there, he took his M.A. degree in the Old Testament and received a Bachelor of Divinity degree in Theology. After seminary training, his first missionary appointment by the Methodist church was in the coal fields of southwest Virginia. There was no church, no members, no parsonage, and no salary; but there were thousands of people who needed spiritual care and that challenge gave him courage.

No preacher had served the territory before, and the people received him almost as someone from another world. The first friend he made was with the local medical doctor, an old-timer who was delighted to have a preacher in the locality. He told the young minister, "Reverend, this mining town needs a man of God. It's pretty tough for these poor souls to eke out any kind of a decent life. They need someone to give them a little hope."

The M.D. proceeded to tell Rev. Crump about one of his most seriously ill patients, an elderly lady living in a shack up on the hill, who wasn't expected to live through the night. "All the relatives from these parts are with her now and I'm sure they'd appreciate having a preacher there at the end." The young minister agreed immediately to go.

Making his way up the hill, he felt a little afraid at the prospect of the woman dying while he was there. Nowhere in his seminary training had he been taught what to do in a situation like this. They had taught him how to translate Hebrew, Greek, and Latin. He had courses in Homiletics, Hermeneutics, and Exegesis, but never once had they told the religious scholar about what to do in a situation the likes of which would confront him in the shack on top of the hill.

Several kerosene lamps provided meager light for the interior of the humble dwelling. Although the two rooms had little furniture, Rev. Crump could see that it was clean and everything was neatly in order. Inwardly, he was trembling but he was able to put on a good front as he greeted and was greeted by the assembled relatives. They showed him into the tiny bedroom where the old lady was surrounded by the female members of her family, paying last respects to the frail figure in the bed.

Tired brown eyes, deep set in a careworn, wrinkled face, stared at him. The old lady managed to wave a few fingers feebly in his direction. He knelt beside her bed and offered a brief prayer as he had been told to do on pastoral visits. Never had anything like this happened in the old lady's life and although it wasn't obvious, she was mightily impressed.

Back in his small, dingy hotel room, the young reverend got out some of his books and started to study up on what to do in case he was called upon to conduct a funeral. The poor woman was at the point of death, and more than likely he would be contacted the next day. His inexperience in these matters weighed heavily on his mind and when he finally went to bed, he tossed and turned for hours until he finally fell into a fitful sleep.

Two days had passed and still no one from the old lady's family contacted him. Surely by this time she must have passed away. The doctor had clearly indicated she probably would go that night he had visited her. That was forty-eight hours ago. Having nothing else to do, he decided to investigate and so Crump headed up the hill on the edge of town once more.

It was a bright and sunny afternoon and as Rev. Crump approached the hut, he could see someone in the yard hoeing the flower bed. As he got closer he stopped in his tracks, not believing his eyes. It was the old lady. As soon as she recognized him, she threw down the hoe and ran out with open arms to greet him, saying, "Oh, here's my preacher again."

Rev. Crump just stood as if he were frozen in his tracks

and listened to her say, "I'm so glad to see you. It was your prayers that got me well." Later, back in his room he wondered what had *really* happened. Was it, indeed, a miracle or just a wonderful accident? He knew there must be a cause for what occurred, and he was going to find out what it was. That incident started him on the great search for Truth.

He had a fruitful ministry in the Methodist church for over twenty-three years, and during this time various strange healing experiences took place, experiences that the minister, with all his scientific background, could not explain. Still, he continued to search for the answer. A member of Rev. Crump's church, a man who for ten years suffered with Parkinson's disease, a dreadful creeping paralysis, was the recipient of one of the minister's numerous healings.

The man was given up not only by leading hospitals in the South but by such renowned institutions as Johns Hopkins and the Mayo Clinic. In fact, he was so pathetic that Crump absolutely hated to visit him for it depressed him so. Then an idea came to the pastor, a *new* idea as to what the victim of Parkinson's disease needed.

It took Rev. Crump just a thirty-minute visit with the patient before the new idea began to manifest. Soon, the paralysis began to leave and new life was felt in limbs long thought incapable of movement. The man had not been to church for over ten years but the very next day, being Sunday, he was there to see if he could actually walk up the steep steps. He was able to do so and the following Sunday he made a heartfelt speech about the "miracle" that took place in his body.

The man was wrong on two points. First, it didn't happen in his body but in his mind; secondly, it wasn't a miracle. Rev. Crump realized that it was the action of some strange inner power and he wanted to know more about it. He had been an engineer and a scientist too long to lose sight of the indisputable fact that everything that happened had a cause.

One day, a local general practitioner who had heard about

the "healin' man," approached Rev. Crump. "Pastor, I've got a patient dying of leukemia who heard about you. She knows I can't do a thing for her, and she begged me to get you to come out. I wish you would, too. She hasn't much time left and your presence would be a great comfort." Rev. Crump was incapable of ignoring such an appeal no matter the time of day or night or how tired he might be.

Arriving at the house, the minister was ushered in by a heavyset man with tobacco-stained whiskers. The elderly woman, he found, was in the depths of despair, pain, and misery. Her face lighted up momentarily when she saw Rev. Crump. "Thank you for coming. I'm so grateful to see you," she said, her voice trembling.

Pulling up a chair next to the bed, Rev. Crump sat down beside her. Intuitively, he started to ask her about her family. "I tell you, Reverend, they're all headed for Hell!" For an hour the words came tumbling out about her husband and six sons and the miserable life she led. It was apparent that she wanted to die and escape her negative environment. Rev. Crump did his best to cheer her up and before he left he ended his visit with a prayer; then he promised that he would return next week to see her.

He came back the following Tuesday, and her husband met him at the door with his fingers to his lips, saying, "Shhhhh, she's in a coma." Everybody was tip-toeing around, whispering. Rev. Crump felt his visit was useless and that he had driven the fifteen miles from the parsonage for nothing, since they refused to let him see her. He started to get mad, and then he demanded that he be allowed to talk to her. Finally, the man agreed. He had never seen a preacher so riled up and it kind of scared him.

The old woman was indeed in a coma. Her face was ashen and her breathing irregular. Rev. Crump walked over to the bed and breaking the silence of the room, leaned over and said, "Well, here's your preacher again. I told you I'd come back to see you again and here I am. I came today because I was leaving town tomorrow and I'll be gone for a couple of weeks. I just wanted to tell you that you'll be getting along fine on THURSDAY."

They all thought the rotund, apple-cheeked minister was crazy. Even though the old lady made no response, he kept right on talking. And this business about her getting better on Thursday, surely the preacher had taken leave of his senses. They didn't know that the reason he told the dying woman she would be healed on Thursday was because he was leaving to attend the great National Conference of Divine Faith Healers up in Pennsylvania, and that on Thursday, when the conference started, he would tell those mighty healers about the woman, and the magic of their prayers would change her back to good health immediately. But what Rev. Crump didn't know was that a tremendous revelation was to come to him through that experience.

He arrived at the healing center after a long and tiresome thousand-mile drive. It was Thursday afternoon and he had planned to get some of the ministers present to pray with him but all were busy checking in and he didn't know anyone personally so he felt it inappropriate to get anyone at that particular time. Soon it was time for supper and, of course, everyone was hungry. And right after the meal the evening program of inspirational songs and messages filled the attention of all. Said Rev. Crump, "I forgot all about the woman I was to pray for."

Sometime later, Rev. Crump made a long-distance telephone call to his wife, letting her know that he arrived safely and that everything was fine. The first thing she said to him was that the sick woman's husband had called her with a message for the minister. Immediately, the churchman thought the message might be for him to return and hold the funeral for he had completely forgotten to pray for her, but his wife continued by reporting: "He told me that this morning they thought she was dead, so they went to the funeral home and selected the casket and completed other details. But when they returned home at noon, she was sitting up and eating dinner. Then the family remembered that this is Thursday, and you told her she would be getting along fine on Thursday, so they wanted to thank you so very, very much."

Rev. Crump felt like sinking through the floor of the telephone booth. He had expected the "magic of prayer" to help the lady, in fact, he had *promised* it; yet, he had forgotten to pray and the seeming miracle had occurred anyway. He couldn't understand what had happened, and this served to intensify his search for the truth. "Of course, now as I look back on it," Rev. Crump readily admits, "anyone studying the philosophy of life found in Concept Therapy not only understands fully what took place but is also capable of performing this healing as well themselves."

He traveled all over the nation looking into various types of spiritual and faith healing. He entered the tents and tabernacles of the great and the not so great, as well as attending healing services in churches of all denominations, from the Shrine of Guadalupe in Mexico to the Shrine of St. Anne de Beaupre in Quebec. "I could see the results of the healing but the *principle* eluded me," he said. "In some instances the healing came about as a result of shouting, rolling, talking in tongues [messages and communications spoken in a language often foreign to the speaker]. In other places it was in complete silence, or perhaps with the hand of the minister on the hand of the patient. Then too, I realized that healing had come about through the years from all kinds of professionals, such as: M.D.'s, osteopaths, chiropractors, naturopaths, naprapaths, etc. It had also been brought about by psychiatrists, psychologists, psychoanalysts, and psychotherapists. I knew there was a thread of Truth that ran through all the healings but I still could not comprehend the principle."

One day, Dr. Glenn Clark, the author of many widely read

books on prayer and healing, and the head of a Spiritual Therapy Prayer Group of national scope, contacted Rev. Crump. He told him that he had heard of Rev. Crump's many healings and that he took the liberty of interviewing many of the people cured by the minister. "I'll tell you this, Rev. Crump; you're dealing with a power that is too high voltage for me to explain, but there is a man in Texas that could possibly explain it," Dr. Clark said.

This information excited Rev. Crump greatly. Perhaps, finally he would be able to solve the mystery. He eagerly questioned Dr. Clark, "Who is this man and what does he teach?" Dr. Clark gladly gave his host the information; information that forever changed the minister's life!

"His name is Fleet, Dr. Thurman Fleet, and he has a big ranch twenty or so miles outside of San Antonio where he teaches something called Concept Therapy," Dr. Clark explained.

Rev. Crump asked, "Did you take this instruction yourself?" Answering, Dr. Clark replied, "I haven't taken the entire course, but I have been exposed to some of it and I heard a lot about the rest from others. It seems this fellow Fleet has apparently been able to perfect a pretty good system of teaching it successfully."

Dr. Fleet was not at all enthusiastic about the prospect of a minister enrolling. I personally suspect that his opinion of much of the clergy, no matter what their denomination might be, was something less than flattering. To discourage this Tennessee preacher, he cooked up some wild stunts in an effort to get him to change his mind about staying. But Dr. Fleet didn't correctly take the measure of the man who would someday become one of his most successful instructors and later be appointed Dean of the Concept Therapy Institute. Rev. Crump stayed.

Another who stayed, after sitting through the instruction, was Dr. Conrad O. Schenk, now President of the Concept

112

Therapy Institute. A graduate of the University of Illinois, his career as a physical education instructor and coach was prematurely halted by a serious neck injury incurred in his college wrestling days. No longer able to earn a living in his regular profession, he remembered that as a high school freshman he had received information from several chiropractic colleges.

Chiropractics intrigued him but his dentist brother was appalled at the very thought. Nevertheless, Connie (as he is called) was most impressed with any healing art that recognized a *universal* and *innate intelligence* within the body that did the healing. "It made terrific sense to me," the ex-coach and athletic instructor said, "and seemed to promise the only logical answer to questions, I realized now, that I had been seeking all my life."

Driven by the need to do something for himself, he cashed in his teacher's pension and enrolled in the Palmer College of Chiropractics. Interestingly enough, the first thing they did was to take X-rays of the cervical region. After fifteen years, a physical cause for the trouble was found. As a result, he started to take adjustments, and after the first one he found that he did not need the glasses that had been prescribed.

It was while practicing chiropractics in Alton, Illinois and still seeking answers that he received a brochure announcing a Concept Therapy class. His first impression was negative. It looked like a cheap piece of advertising material to him but something in the copy of the folder struck him. It had to do with the phrase *contacting and directing the innate,* and the word *Soul* also stood out.

It was in the early forties when Conrad O. Schenk, D.C. drove to St. Louis and first took Concept Therapy. About the third day of the five-day course (classes for laymen are now only two and one-half days) something within began to say, "This is it, this is it!" Dr. Schenk had finally found the answers to all the questions he had been seeking. Here was a practical, *workable*, scientific way of life.

He had no intention of leaving his practice in the Prairie State to teach, but a couple of years later, during a review class in Fort Worth, Dr. Fleet made a statement that he needed someone to help him teach a Concept Therapy class scheduled for Los Angeles. About a dozen or so advanced students of the work, including Dr. Schenk, were sitting around the hotel's coffee shop table at the conclusion of the day's session, and almost as if it were a "cooked-up" plot, they said in unison, "Why not use Schenk?"

Dr. Fleet, with an expression of pure innocence on his face, replied, "Say, that's a fine idea. What about it, Connie, will you help me teach the class?" Dr. Schenk agreed and that was the beginning of his career in Concept Therapy, a career which led him to the Institute's presidency in 1961. And on that July 30th afternoon at Aum Sat Tat ranch in Texas, when his peers unanimously selected him to lead Concept Therapy, one of those present was Dr. Bernard Higdon who, along with his charming wife, Myra, is an important mainstay of the movement.

The soft-spoken, balding instructor known for his quick wit couldn't help but think back to a time when the name Schenk on a penny-post card was instrumental in changing his life. Bernard Higdon, graduate of St. Johns prep school in Washington, D.C. and the Massachusetts State College in Amherst, never gave much thought to philosophy. His area of interest centered around horticulture and landscape architecture. He parlayed that interest into a successful business, the Capital Nursery in Washington, D.C. Then one terrible day he fell to the floor of his greenhouse, paralyzed from the shoulders down. He exhausted his funds on medical specialists but after several years he still remained incapacitated. "Try to make the best of it, Mr. Higdon. There's not much hope that you can be helped," the physicians and surgeons told him.

Against his will, a friend took him to see a chiropractor. Higdon couldn't believe it, but after a few sessions he could feel himself getting a little better. "Doctor, what is doing it?" he wanted to know. "What is causing the healing?"

The chiropractor, an old gentleman who wholeheartedly believed in his calling, answered, "I only adjust the bones like I was taught, Mr. Higdon. I don't really know what it is that does the healing."

That caused Bernard Higdon to do a lot of thinking and a lot of revaluating. He was grateful for the return of his health, and he felt he wanted to help others as he had been helped. He decided to embark on a new profession, chiropractics. After extensive training, he opened an office in a small Florida town and it wasn't long before he was once again enjoying success; yet, one question would constantly arise in his mind, "Why can I heal some patients and not others?"

He could not resolve his failures. His line of reasoning went: "If I'm truly working with a science and my instructors taught me that I was, then why doesn't it follow through and be consistent in every case?" Even though he was once again financially secure, living in a beautiful home, earning the respect of the townspeople, something gnawed at him, refusing to go away. "Why can't I be content?" he wondered. "What is the purpose and meaning of my life anyway?"

It was an ordinary-looking advertisement-bearing postcard that arrived with a batch of daily mail. Dr. Higdon gave it a cursory glance and was about to throw it away with the rest of the junk-mail when something inclined him not to. Later that day, he dug it out of his pocket and reread the announcement of a forthcoming informative lecture to be given by a Dr. Conrad O. Schenk.

He arrived at the hotel lecture room early, thinking that he would avoid the possibility of not getting a seat. To his surprise, he found that only eight others had bothered to show up, but the empty chairs didn't seem to affect the speaker.

Higdon was impressed with what he heard that night but he decided against enrolling in the forthcoming class.

A week after the lecture, an eight-year-old girl was brought to Dr. Higdon's office. The parents admitted that their child, seriously ill, had not been helped by a succession of M.D.'s, osteopaths, chiropractors, and even faith healers. Dr. Higdon was thought of only as a last hope. He didn't mind this and confidently accepted the case, since he knew that he had exceptionally good luck with children.

"Don't worry, your little girl will be fine," he told the parents. Weeks passed and his apprehension became more and more pronounced as his little patient failed to respond to the treatment. He was beside himself, confidence gone and incapable of clear thinking about the case. "Why isn't she getting better?" he continually asked himself. "What am I doing wrong?"

Unable to stand it any longer, he made copies of the child's X-rays and prepared duplicates of her case history. He airmailed the material to four of the nation's leading chiropractic colleges with an urgent appeal for immediate diagnosis and suggested treatment. All four schools replied within the week, but to Higdon's horror each diagnosed the problem completely different than the others and each suggested completely different treatments.

Now he was really confused, utterly and hopelessly befuddled, not knowing which way to turn, and all the while the little girl was edging closer and closer to the end. Then he remembered something this fellow Schenk had said in that Concept Therapy informative lecture; something about how to give a healing suggestion. Could he do it and would it work? He had to try and he did. In two weeks, the child was on the road to recovery. Success . . . it was never sweeter.

Dr. Higdon's amazement was great; he had not even taken the Concept Therapy course and he already had immensely benefited from it. When the class in a Miami hotel commenced, he was sitting in the front row center. What he heard convinced him, and later his wife, that this teaching could benefit all of mankind. The purpose of his life now became clear. The path he must follow was at once self-evident. Like the others, he never looked back; his gaze fixed to a far point on the summit.

# CHAPTER ELEVEN

## Three More Who Stayed

No one would dare call him Oma Winfield Whittenberg; always, it's O.W., or Dr. Whittenberg. He celebrated his eightieth birthday looking forward to the Concept Therapy class he was planning to teach the following week. A handsome man with crystal-clear, ice-blue eyes and a shock of snow-white hair, he stands erect and alert. O.W. is an impressive figure in front of any class, and always at his side his beloved Myrtle; wife, teaching partner, and detail "carry-outer."

There seemed to be a thread of continuity linking all the chiropractors in Concept Therapy that I talked to. That goes for the medical doctors in the work, as well. Always the question that haunts them is: "What *heals?*" And so it was with O.W., a chiropractor since 1914. For thirty years he sought an answer to no avail. Finally, after three decades of treating disease, he decided to try and find a way to maintain health. "I observed case after case who regained health as if by magic or miracles," he said. "No one could explain how or what had happened to create the change."

Like so many others before him, Dr. Whittenberg received a notice of a Concept Therapy class; this one to be held in Milwaukee. And like so many others, he immediately threw it aside and continued with his busy schedule. Again, following a familiar pattern, when he reached home and was about to retire for the evening, he began to think about the experiences of the day and a statement he read on the postcard announcement of the Concept Therapy class. "We teach the laws by which health is restored and maintained." The more those words ran through his mind, the more excited he became. "Of course, that's it! The *laws* of healing, that's what I need to learn," he fairly shouted to the bedroom walls.

Knowing he *had* to investigate, when morning came he was on the telephone trying to convince several doctor friends to come to the class with him. Three of his colleagues agreed and so the four of them flew down to Milwaukee for the instruction. Recalling his first class in 1945, Dr. Whittenberg said, "I enjoyed what I heard very much but I honestly didn't feel I received the answer I was looking for. Later, I was to understand that I didn't as yet have the 'brain cells' for receiving the answers given in that class."

What he did get in the Concept Therapy class was a strong desire to continue study of the subject. A year later, he helped to organize a class in Minneapolis so that members of his family and friends could secure this knowledge, and perhaps in time they would assist him in getting his full answer. "I didn't know it then, but I now had 'cells of recognition' and it was in this review class that I got my fundamental answer," Dr. Whittenberg remembered. "I clearly saw that the source of all healing must come from life . . . that only through the changing of the expression if this great *Conscious Power* to normal could health exist."

Knowing the answer was one thing, but demonstrating it was another matter, admits Dr. Whittenberg. He made the decision to sell his Minneapolis practice and open up an office in Texas so that he could more easily get the necessary training in the use of this new philosophy. His practice in Texas flourished as he perfected his ability to properly use Concept Therapy. In 1949, he decided to retire. It was at this time that Aum Sat Tat ranch was opened as an international home for members of the Concept Therapy philosophy. "It was indeed a surprise when we had completed our retirement home on the ranch that I was appointed a staff member, to be trained by Dr. Fleet. We were trained not only in the operation of the institution and its policies but also as teachers of the Concept Therapy philosophy . . . thus, my retirement became one of the busiest and most enlightening periods of my entire life," Dr. Whittenberg happily said.

Myrtle Whittenberg, many years her husband's junior, shared the joy of O.W.'s "retirement." She too has said over and over, "I've never been so busy in all my life, but I love it." When I asked her the question, "What brought you in to Concept Therapy?" she answered, "My search for the answers to Life." As you can clearly see, these Concept Therapists are an inquisitive lot, unwilling to remain in ignorance. As much restlessness and, sometimes, pain that this "Divine Discontent" brings, it is a common and God-given trait that all true seekers share.

"We were poor, I mean poverty-stricken. I was a sickly child from birth, one of eleven children. Illness and death were no strangers in my family. Perhaps this made me cry out for answers that could change my hellish existence," Myrtle Whittenberg said, recalling her childhood with not the slightest trace of bitterness. "Strangely enough, none of my brothers or sisters ever questioned the reason for the circumstances and experiences as I did." The other children seemed to be satisfied with the orthodox teachings of their church, which, so far as Myrtle was concerned, gave no logical explanation for her family's circumstance, except to say, "It is God's will that it be so."

Many times, young little Myrtle's reasoning bordered on the blasphemous, or so her elders accused. A parent of one of her school chums was shocked to hear the youngster spout, "We are put here by a God whom we are told is *all good*; this *all good being*, who Jesus said would bring us life abundantly, has instead filled our home with bad. Mom and Dad are both

120

sick. More babies are being born and then die before they're a year old. We're told to pray and I do pray, but nothing has changed, why?"

Disaster followed Myrtle to adulthood. And one gloomy, heartbreaking day, she had been diagnosed by the family physician as having cancer. Through the recommendation of a friend, she became a patient of Dr. Whittenberg who, in time, cured her completely. O.W. found a fertile mind, eager for the truth, and so he told her about Concept Therapy. For the very first time life made sense. The transformation that took place in Myrtle's life was more "miraculous" than the healing of her cancer.

"You can't imagine what a revelation it was to learn that by living in conformity with the Universal Laws, I could gain the worthwhile things of life," Mrs. Whittenberg said, and she was speaking from the depths of her heart. "It became very clear to me that the reasons for the hardships of my good parents were due to their lack of knowledge concerning the principles of living life. They had no understanding of how to consciously contact God . . . the God within . . . and communicate with it."

Myrtle was convinced that this teaching was the answer to not only the problems and questions of seeking individuals but to those of the whole world. She has often said, "I felt so fortunate to have had the great privilege of gaining this precious knowledge that I wanted others to have it; others who were perhaps also confused."

Another member of the distaff side, to become convinced of Concept Therapy's great value in the field of human affairs, was attractive, talented (an accomplished singer and skilled platform speaker, as well as an able administrator and executive secretary) Katherine Calhoun. Born in Virginia, her parents moved to Nashville, Tennessee when she was a child and there she grew up.

She was interested in religious endeavors and did considerable postgraduate work toward becoming a certified

Director of Religious Education in the Methodist Church. While serving in East Tennessee, she heard about Concept Therapy and what she heard intrigued her. Upon learning that a national Concept Therapy convention was scheduled to be held in San Antonio in July of 1950, she was determined to attend.

The feeling she received at the convention (just question anyone who has ever attended a Concept Therapy convention and you'll understand how tremendously "high" the "vibrations" can be) led her to enroll in the first possible class. "It seemed that all the longing, seeking, striving, waiting, and yearning of my life was answered in that which I felt during the convention, and indeed, I could call it the *answer* to the *mystery of life* for me," she related, her eyes glistening.

She resigned from her church position, although her plans were by no means specific. She had an idea in back of her mind about getting further Concept Therapy training at Aum Sat Tat in Texas but nothing was certain. She hadn't mentioned it to anyone; it was just a possibility. Then she received a letter from Dr. Fleet offering her a secretarial position at the Concept Therapy Institute.

Katherine Calhoun was able to take advantage of the opportunity to listen to the many ranch lectures. The "jam sessions" at night were particularly helpful and inspiring. The long meditation periods (the SLUMP) of music each evening provided needed time for soul-searching and planning her life.

Katherine frankly admits that, "Before Concept Therapy, my body had been wracked with physical ailments and I was constantly under the care of four or five doctors all at the same time, each one specializing in treating one of my ailments. I was taking from ten to twenty allergy shots per day. I was allergic to about fifty or so things, such as: chocolate candy, ice cream, animals, wool, dust, perfume, nylon, and a variety of foods. I owed about a thousand dollars in doctor bills."

The thing that really had Kathy worried was the possibility

she might be going blind. Her vision was becoming worse every day. Besides this she was bothered with digestive disturbances, eliminative troubles, hemorrhoids, headaches, and glandular aches and pains. "As soon as I understood the basic principles taught in Concept Therapy I realized where certain basic *Laws of Life* were being broken, and in many instances the very ones who were supposed to help me were actually causing me to "break other laws," she points out.

"I began to *know myself* and the *power* which was striving to express itself perfectly through me. As I gradually attained this *awareness* my troubles began to disappear rapidly," Kathy is happy to report. "And now, I consider myself to be one of the healthiest persons in the world."

She more than likely is right, for at present Katherine Calhoun is busily engaged in holding lectures and teaching Concept Therapy classes almost every day. When she isn't doing classroom work or tending to numerous administrative details, she is out contacting people, ten to eighteen hours a day. This now has been her schedule for the past fifteen years.

"As I look back over the decade and a half of teaching Concept Therapy, each class revealed new truths and each holds its own precious memories that nothing can erase. People come into each class borne down by loads of negative thinking; wrong things, and wrong acts, and in the short space of less than three days they learn to know what's wrong and are inspired to know and do that which is right," Kathy solemnly told me. "The *change* that takes place within them in one short weekend is worth all the effort it takes."

Few people realize that sometimes it costs more to put on a class than the teachers receive through tuition. Ask any instructor and you'll quickly be told that the real compensation for teaching Concept Therapy is seeing the transformation that takes place in the lives of the students "who get *the big idea* . . . the *idea* that they are *one* with the *Infinite Power* and that it is trying to express itself perfectly through them if they only learn how to cooperate with it properly."

I wholeheartedly agree with Katherine Calhoun when she says, "There is no price tag that can be placed on the peace, contentment, satisfaction, health-giving qualities, and a *feeling* of being at home in the Universe . . . which have come to me from my studies of Concept Therapy. It is indeed the treasure which a man found in the field and went straightway and sold all that he had, to buy that field. This expresses what Concept Therapy symbolizes to me."